OPEN MARKETS MATTER

THE BENEFITS OF TRADE AND INVESTMENT LIBERALISATION

ORGANISATION FOR ECONOMIC CO-OPERATION AND DEVELOPMENT

ORGANISATION FOR ECONOMIC CO-OPERATION AND DEVELOPMENT

Pursuant to Article 1 of the Convention signed in Paris on 14th December 1960, and which came into force on 30th September 1961, the Organisation for Economic Co-operation and Development (OECD) shall promote policies designed:
- to achieve the highest sustainable economic growth and employment and a rising standard of living in Member countries, while maintaining financial stability, and thus to contribute to the development of the world economy;
- to contribute to sound economic expansion in Member as well as non-member countries in the process of economic development; and
- to contribute to the expansion of world trade on a multilateral, non-discriminatory basis in accordance with international obligations.

The original Member countries of the OECD are Austria, Belgium, Canada, Denmark, France, Germany, Greece, Iceland, Ireland, Italy, Luxembourg, the Netherlands, Norway, Portugal, Spain, Sweden, Switzerland, Turkey, the United Kingdom and the United States. The following countries became Members subsequently through accession at the dates indicated hereafter: Japan (28th April 1964), Finland (28th January 1969), Australia (7th June 1971), New Zealand (29th May 1973), Mexico (18th May 1994), the Czech Republic (21st December 1995), Hungary (7th May 1996), Poland (22nd November 1996) and Korea (12th December 1996). The Commission of the European Communities takes part in the work of the OECD (Article 13 of the OECD Convention).

Publié en français sous le titre :

POUR L'OUVERTURE DES MARCHÉS :
LES AVANTAGES DE LA LIBÉRALISATION DES ÉCHANGES
ET DE L'INVESTISSEMENT

PREFACE

BY DONALD J. JOHNSTON,
SECRETARY-GENERAL OF THE OECD

When they met last May, Ministers of our Member governments asked the OECD Secretariat to prepare a study on the benefits of trade and investment liberalisation. We have done so, and this book is the outcome of our work.

It could hardly have been more timely. More people than ever the world over are sharing the tangible gains from liberalisation. Yet there are growing doubts and anxieties among citizens about the consequences of that liberalisation process.

Such a paradox is understandable, given the pace and depth of current economic and social change. It also underlines the urgency of responding to those public anxieties. This study is a contribution to that response.

There are two key messages in this book.

First, there is a pressing need to communicate what trade and investment can and cannot do and what liberalisation is and is not responsible for.

Liberalisation brings clear net benefits for our societies. This book endeavours to identify and explain them, in as objective a way as possible. It is vital that those essential benefits are well understood. At the same time, liberalisation is not the most important cause of transformation in our economies. Many other factors are in play, most notably technology-driven structural change. Nor is liberalisation an end in itself. It is a part – albeit an important one – of a whole set of policies aimed at bringing well-being to our societies and citizens.

Second, we must respond to the concerns of those citizens who are – or who perceive themselves to be – adversely affected by those changes, whether they are driven by trade and investment liberalisation or by other factors.

As this study points out, protection is not the answer. It inevitably translates into more protracted – and more costly – adjustment. What is needed are policies targeted at the root of the problem. The OECD Jobs Strategy and the OECD Recommendations on Regulatory Reform point the way. There is a need for labour market policies that provide adequate income security while facilitating reemployment of displaced workers in sectors which are growing. More fundamentally, governments need to work on a whole range of policies, such as education, training, taxation, and product market flexibility that can help citizens and communities to adjust – not only to market openness, but to all the factors driving structural change in our economies.

I am confident that if we apply these key messages effectively, we will be in a better position to consolidate the gains from trade and investment liberalisation. It is vital that we do so. The last fifty years have shown how such liberalisation can contribute to prosperity and well-being. The challenge now is to spread the message of how it can actually meet the needs of our citizens in the future.

DONALD J. JOHNSTON
APRIL 1998

ACKNOWLEDGEMENTS

Joanna R. Shelton assumed overall responsibility for this project as Deputy Secretary-General. Drafting of the book and project coordination was undertaken by the Trade Directorate, under the management of Gerhard Abel and Crawford Falconer. Pierre Sauvé served as lead drafter, with significant additional contributions from Rachel Thompson and Barbara Fliess. Substantive inputs were also provided by Jacques de Miramon, Dale Andrew, Raed Safadi, Didier Campion and Karsten Steinfatt. Gloria O'Hara, with assistance from Sarah Cameron Nee, Ann Katoh and Elsie Lotthé, spared no effort in preparing the text for publication. Marie-Laure Caille was instrumental in getting the web page up and running.

The book's preparation drew on and benefited from valuable contributions from several parts of the Secretariat. These included comments and inputs from *Deputy Secretaries-General* (Kumiharu Shigehara and Thorvald Moe) as well as from the *Directorate for Food, Agriculture and Fisheries* (Gérard Viatte, Carmel Cahill, Leo Maier and Eirikur Einarsson); the *Directorate for Financial, Fiscal and Enterprise Affairs* (William Witherell, Pierre Poret and Stephen Thomsen); the *Directorate for Education, Employment, Labour and Social Affairs* (John Martin, Peter Schwanse, Peter Scherer, Paul Swaim and Willem Adema); the *Development Centre* (Ulrich Hiemenz, Kiichiro Fukasaku and Helmut Reisen); the *Development Co-operation Directorate* (Bernard Wood, Stéphanie Baile and Bill Nicol); the *Directorate for Science, Technology and Industry* (Risaburo Nezu, Daniel Malkin and Thomas Hatzichronoglou); the *Environment Directorate* (Joke Waller-Hunter, Michel Potier, Jan Adams and Tom Jones); the *Economics Department* (Michael Feiner, Sveinbjörn Blöndal and Ann Vourc'h); the *General Secretariat* (Andrew Dean and Tony Rottier); the *Legal Directorate* (David Small); the *Public Affairs and Communications Directorate* (Chris Brooks, Denis Lamb, Catherine Habib, Lisa Williams, Emmanuel Dalmenesche and Patrick Gavignet); and the *Territorial Development Service* (Mario Pezzini). As the work proceeded it also benefited from the advice and comment provided by Delegations in the Trade Committee.

TABLE OF CONTENTS

EXECUTIVE SUMMARY

This study responds to the request of OECD Ministers at the May 1997 Ministerial Meeting that the Secretariat produce a *"focused, multidisciplinary study of the benefits of trade and investment liberalisation"*. The study documents the contribution of trade and investment liberalisation to wealth-creation and well-being. But it also addresses and puts into perspective the concern that open markets are responsible for a variety of ills that afflict our societies and trouble our citizens.

The study's chief purpose is to help governments better explain the clear net benefits of keeping markets open to international trade and investment and of staying the course of market-led reforms. In doing so, it stresses that market liberalisation is not a self-contained, abstract end in itself. Rather, it is one important component of what must be a coherent set of policies aimed at achieving a durable improvement in living standards. It is also recognised that, while there are clear overall benefits for our societies, it is necessary to adopt properly designed and well-targeted policies to assist those who are harmed by change.

THE BENEFITS OF OPEN MARKETS

Trade and foreign direct investment are major engines of growth in developed and developing countries alike. The volume of world merchandise trade is 16 times greater today than it was in 1950. That reflects the dismantling of import and export barriers. Outflows of foreign direct investment (FDI) have grown even faster, rising twenty-five fold during the last quarter century, from $14 billion to $350 billion a year. Trade and investment-induced market integration has led to deeper forms of economic interdependence among nations, as a growing number of developing and former centrally-planned economies have become more closely linked to the global economy.

The case for open markets rests on solid foundations. One of these is the fact that when individuals and companies engage in specialisation and exchange, a country will exploit its comparative advantage. It will devote its natural, human, industrial and financial resources to their highest and best uses. This will provide gains to firms and consumers alike. Another is the strong preference of people the world over for more, rather than less, freedom of choice.

A more open domestic market is not a handicap; it is a source of competitive strength. Exposure to international trade is a powerful stimulus to efficiency. Efficiency, in turn, contributes to economic growth and rising incomes.

Results speak for themselves. In the last decade, countries that have been more open have achieved double the annual average growth of others. Liberalisation from the Uruguay Round alone has delivered a global tax cut estimated to be worth more than $200 billion per annum: the equivalent of adding a new Korea or Switzerland to the world economy over the next ten years. Liberalisation benefits citizens in tangible ways: in the case of Australia, for example, its recent unilateral trade liberalisation has, in effect, put A$ 1,000 in the hands of the average Australian family.

The case for opening markets to investment is as compelling as it is for trade. More open economies enjoy higher rates of private investment, which is a major determinant of economic growth. FDI is actively courted by countries, not least because it generates spillovers such as improved management and better technology.

The benefits are tangible. As is true with firms that trade, firms and sectors with high

FDI have higher average labour productivity and pay higher wages. Outward investment enables firms to remain competitive and thus supports employment at home. Investment abroad stimulates exports of machinery and other capital goods, and increases demand for intermediary products, know-how and specialised services. A study of OECD countries found that each $1.00 of outward foreign direct investment was associated with $2.00 of *additional* exports, and a trade surplus of $1.70. Without FDI those exports would be smaller, sustaining fewer of the more productive, better paying jobs that go with them.

Liberalisation can benefit both developed and developing countries alike. As is the case for OECD countries, foreign investment brings higher wages, and is a major source of technology transfer and managerial skills in host developing countries. This contributes to rising prosperity in the developing countries concerned, as well as enhancing demand for higher value-added exports from OECD economies. In this way, developing countries are becoming major stake-holders in the trading system today, as is evidenced by estimates that close to one half of Uruguay Round welfare gains may accrue to them.

HOW DOES MARKET OPENNESS AFFECT EMPLOYMENT AND EARNINGS?

Despite these gains, concerns are voiced about the impact of openness on labour markets. This is seen to stem from the fact that, since the 1970s there has been an increasing differential between labour market outcomes – employment and earnings – of skilled and unskilled workers in OECD countries. This has led some to see competition, particularly from low wage, low-labour-standard developing countries, as the fundamental cause of this situation.

This study finds that the negative effects of such trade and investment are, at most, modest. Adverse effects in labour markets are primarily driven by changes in technology and business organisation. The fact is that these and other changes such as those arising from domestic competition, shifts in patterns of demand and movement in the business cycle occur continuously in modern economies. Thus, the effects of trade and investment need to be kept in perspective. This is why, in the case of the United States, trade has been found to be responsible for less than 6 per cent of the drop in US manufacturing employment between 1978-90. The following factors should also be borne in mind:

- While it is recognised that trade, investment and technological change have interacted in ways that depress demand for unskilled workers, competition from low wage countries has not been a major contributing factor. Fully 80 to 90 per cent of changes in wages and income distribution in OECD countries are the result of factors other than trade with developing countries.

- While imports of manufactured goods from emerging economies have grown over the past three decades, their value amounts to a mere 1.6 per cent of OECD countries' combined output. The fact is that total trade of manufactures between OECD countries and emerging economies is broadly in balance, a situation that has changed little since the late 1960s. This draws attention to the mutual benefits of such exchanges.

- Developed economies today derive around 70 per cent of their output and employment from the service sector. Most of these services remain non-tradable and, to the extent that there is competitive pressure associated with greater trade and investment in services, this comes from other predominantly high wage OECD countries.

- Increased foreign direct investment and the outsourcing of production exert at most modest effects on OECD labour markets. As with trade, FDI is still largely an intra-

OECD affair. Some 85 per cent of outflows originate in, and 65 per cent of inflows are directed at, other high-wage, high producing OECD countries. A good 60 per cent of world FDI flows is directed to, and sustains employment in, services activities where OECD countries and workers are by far the most competitive suppliers. In addition, the FDI that flows outside OECD tends to go to the largest or richest markets rather than those that could be considered "low wage platforms".

■ The aggregate contribution of trade to employment has to be taken into account too. Since 1993, exports have accounted for one-third of US economic growth and one in ten civilian jobs are supported by exports of goods and services. The ratio in manufacturing is one in five. In Ireland, one in four jobs depend on exports; in Canada, it is one in three.

Despite the fact that open trade and investment produces overall gains, some citizens and communities (often concentrated in particular sectors) experience adjustment pains and income losses as a result of liberalisation. This presents a genuine challenge to our societies. The real question is what is the appropriate response?

THE COST OF PROTECTIONISM

One approach has been – and remains – to protect industry and workers against imports by raising trade barriers. Societies typically pay a high price when they resort to protectionism. Protectionism raises the price of both imports and domestic products, which restricts consumer choice and places the heaviest burden on those in society who are least well off. It slows change and raises its cost, inflicts damage on exporting firms by making them less competitive, and almost invariably translates into greater long-term hardship.

Protectionism does not deliver what it promises. In the United States, it has been estimated that if liberalisation were stopped right now, the wages of skilled workers would decline 2 - 5 per cent and unskilled wages would remain flat. Imposing a 30 per cent tariff on developing country exports would inflict even greater damage; it would cut unskilled wages by 1 per cent and skilled wages by 5 per cent.

The cost to consumers of protectionism in OECD countries has been estimated to be as much as US$300 billion. The average cost to consumers of a job protected exceeds the wages of employees whose jobs are saved. In one case the consumer cost of saving a single job in one OECD country was estimated to be as high as US$600,000 per annum. Even when the cost is lower, the fact remains that protectionism consumes resources that could more fruitfully be used to retrain or provide transitional income support to displaced workers, or to develop new products or new businesses.

HOW TO DEAL EFFECTIVELY WITH THE NEED FOR ADJUSTMENT

The fact that resorting to protectionism is not the answer is a vital message in its own right. But it is not the whole story. Policies are still needed to ease the plight of those in the front line of adjustment. There is a need to respond to concerns about distributional issues and the transitional costs arising from that adjustment. It is just as important to stress that there is, in fact, a better way.

Properly designed labour market and social policies that provide adequate income security, while facilitating the redeployment of displaced workers into expanding firms and sectors, produce important equity and efficiency gains. The effectiveness of these policies will, of course, depend on the degree of flexibility in labour markets, as well as on a range of other policies. In fact, a much broader strategy is called for, one capable of upgrading the skills of workers and raising workforce mobility. Areas such as education, training, taxation, pension reform and the portability of health benefits (where that is an issue) need to be dealt with in a comprehensive way. In addition, introducing greater product market flexibility through well-structured regulatory reform can help firms remain competitive in the face of tougher competition. These steps will ensure that citizens and communities are able to take advantage of, and adjust to what is the foremost challenge they face; namely, technology-driven structural change.

In sum, a balanced mix of policies is needed to reinforce adaptive capacity in the face of *all* structural changes, including those stemming from trade and investment liberalisation. The OECD Jobs Strategy sets out the ways to deal with these issues.

Social protection policies also need to be reoriented to ensure that those who lose their jobs – including as a result of trade or investment liberalisation – are insured against excessive income loss during the period of search for a new job. There is no inevitable connection between increased openness and less social protection. In fact, increased international trade and investment is an additional reason to improve the efficiency of public social protection systems, rather than a rationale for reducing them.

In regard to concerns about core labour standards, it seems clear that this issue – vital as it is – does not call into question the fundamentals of trade and investment liberalisation. Rather, it is a matter of finding the most effective way to ensure implementation of those core standards. OECD studies have concluded that low standards are not generally a significant competitive factor in trade with the countries concerned; and there tends to be a positive association over time between sustained trade liberalisation and improvements in core labour standards. At the same time, OECD work has found that concerns expressed by certain developing countries that core standards would negatively affect their economic performance or their international position also are unfounded; indeed it is theoretically possible that the observance of core standards would strengthen the long term economic performance of all countries.

IS TRADE AND INVESTMENT LIBERALISATION INIMICAL TO ENVIRONMENTAL PROTECTION?

There are concerns that liberalisation of trade and investment may be fundamentally inimical to the environment or will lead to a "race to the bottom" in environmental standards. The fear is that developed nations will be pressured to relax, or precluded from improving, their environmental standards in the face of competitive pressure from developing countries with lower environmental standards and that firms will relocate to take advantage of lower environmental standards in developing countries.

Trade and investment liberalisation, by promoting a more efficient use of resources and sustaining growth, can make a vital contribution towards creating the conditions necessary for environmental improvement. The evidence shows that there is a positive link between countries' environmental performance and rising per capita income levels, security of property rights and administrative efficiency. That is reflected, for example, in the fact that standards for air and water quality in OECD countries are much higher today than they were fifty years ago, and it is these countries that today apply the most stringent environmental regulations.

Trade and investment liberalisation is, of course, only a part of the overall growth process, but it can clearly play a vital contributing part, fuelling the improvement in environmental quality that has gone with it. It can do so by promoting a more efficient allocation of resources (including environmental resources), removing restrictions and distortions (e.g. subsidies) that are damaging to the environment and improving the speedier transfer, adoption and diffusion of environmentally friendly technologies.

The wealth creation to which liberalisation contributes should also help reduce poverty, which is often the underlying cause of environmental degradation in many developing countries. It may also provide the means to pay for the prevention or clean-up of pollution. Studies show that pollution intensity has grown most rapidly in those countries that remained most closed to world market forces. In turn, this lends support to the view that openness to foreign competition is more likely to increase the demand for improved, rather than lower, environmental standards.

There have been concerns that, with liberalisation, investors will be increasingly attracted by "pollution havens". There can, of course, be exceptional cases of this kind. However, experience shows that openness to trade and investment generally translates into increased pressures for more stringent environmental standards. Moreover, multi-national firms are adopting world-wide standards for environmental performance. It should also be borne in mind that over 60 per cent of FDI takes place in less pollution-intensive service industries and that already the amount of investment in pollution-intensive industries in developing countries is lower as a share of total FDI than it was in 1972.

Of course, the concern that economic growth should not harm the environment is real, and the need to avoid this is imperative. But it is vital to target the actual policies and situations that are the problem and to tailor the responses accordingly. Trade and investment liberalisation are not the root causes of environmental problems. Under trade agreements such as the WTO, governments retain the sovereign right to set their own environmental objectives. And they can apply measures to enforce achievement of them within their territories – just as long as they are not more trade restrictive than necessary and they do not apply a double standard by discriminating against the commerce of other countries. In fact, the real problems that arise can in many cases be traced to situations where the use of environmental resources is not properly priced and reflected in the prices of goods and services consumed by firms and people. What is needed, however, is not a halt to liberalisation efforts, but sound environmental policies that are properly integrated with trade and investment policies.

While the demand for environmental quality is likely to rise as societies move up the income ladder, this is not inevitable. Neither is there any guarantee that significant improvements in environmental quality will be demanded early enough in the development path to cut the pollution intensity of production fast. Nor can we ignore the risk that liberalisation of trade and investment may exacerbate problems, if environmental policies are poorly designed or weakly enforced. But that does not mean there is any reason to retreat from liberalisation. On the contrary, it underlines the fact that countries need to have adequate environmental policies and infrastructure in place to address the environmental effects of economic growth generally, and that coherent and mutually supportive trade, investment and environment policies are of paramount importance.

HOW DOES MARKET OPENNESS AFFECT NATIONAL SOVEREIGNTY?

There are concerns in some quarters about the way in which market openness affects national sovereignty. More particularly, there are concerns that increasing trade and investment flows, and multilateral rules for trade and investment, may erode the capacity of governments to exercise national "regulatory" sovereignty. That is, to decide the appropriate policies and regulatory approaches for their own country or region, on issues such as environmental protection or consumer health and safety, as well as on trade and investment matters. There is also a perception that multilateral agreements encourage or even require such regulatory standards to be reduced or eliminated.

Trade and investment liberalisation, in fact, forms part of overall strategies to maintain and even strengthen a country's capacity to determine its own future (and thus its sovereignty), by improving its competitiveness and income, and making it less vulnerable to external shocks. Thus liberalisation and regulatory reform are undertaken by national governments (whether unilaterally or in the context of international negotiations between sovereign governments) to enhance national interests. Such decisions are made precisely in order to gain the added security, stability and enhanced prospects for national welfare, that internationally agreed rules provide. An agreement such as the WTO is essentially an *exercise* of national sovereignty rather than a *surrender* of it.

Multilateral trade and investment agreements do *not* regard all national regulatory measures as unnecessary. Nor do they require the removal or reduction of all barriers to foreign trade and investment. Indeed, governments retain the sovereign right to set their own objectives on such matters. The rules do require countries to prepare, implement and administer national regulations that affect foreign goods, services and investment in a transparent, non-arbitrary and non-discriminatory way. But that is because governments have taken a sovereign decision to abide by such rules. And they have done so because they recognise that discriminating between foreign and domestic firms is rarely, if ever, necessary to achieve domestic policy goals; and that such rules help promote fairness and stability in an international economy in which all countries have a stake. Such agreements explicitly provide that high-quality effective national regulation be permitted to work properly in a number of areas. Where the rules place limits on recourse to certain trade or investment restrictions, this arises from the agreement of sovereign member countries that it is in their mutual interest to have each other do so. Moreover, the WTO rules and dispute settlement processes recognise that there can be legitimate grounds for exceptions from these rules in certain circumstances, or to achieve other policy objectives.

WHAT IS THE ROLE OF POLITICS AND LEADERSHIP?

Past experience makes it clear that liberalisation should be sustained in order to continue to improve the living standards of our citizens. More open economies typically grow faster, and the rising incomes they provide are likely, on balance, to provide greater freedom of choice, as well as greater efficiency. At the same time, proponents of market opening need to devote more time and effort to addressing concerns about trade and investment liberalisation. Efforts must also be made to explain that pressures on jobs and incomes or on the environment are best dealt with through targeted and co-ordinated policies addressing the problems at their root. Protectionist responses almost always make matters worse.

The liberalisation debate is a debate over ideas, and it matters greatly that OECD Member governments be in a position to communicate why and how market liberalisation forms part of the answer to the concerns of citizens, rather than being their root cause.

The immediacy of pains that liberalisation can generate and the more diffuse, longer-term, manner in which its benefits tend to materialise for economies as a whole, will always complicate the lives of advocates of market openness. Done properly, liberal trade and investment are, and must be seen as being, not only about prosperity and greater freedom of choice but also about fairness. Fairness in ensuring that the general interest – concern for the welfare of *all* citizens – prevails over special interests; and in seeing to it that the dividends of liberalisation are distributed more equitably, both within and between countries. This is why the politics and exercise of leadership at the national and international level continues to matter greatly.

INTRODUCTION

This study responds to the request of OECD Ministers that the Organisation produce a *"focused, multidisciplinary study of the benefits of trade and investment liberalisation"*.[1] The call by Ministers for a study on the economy-wide benefits of trade and investment liberalisation is most opportune, coming as it does at a time when negotiations on a Multilateral Agreement on Investment are under way; and a few weeks ahead of the world community's celebration in May 1998 of five decades of progress on the multilateral trade front as embodied in the GATT and now the WTO. The study's chief purpose is to help Member country governments in their task of communicating the clear net benefits to society of keeping markets open to international trade and investment and of staying the course of market-led reforms.[2]

We live in a time of paradox. There can scarcely have been a time when so many countries from so many different parts of the world at such different levels of development were involved in so many fora on so many policy and rule-making initiatives aimed at progressively rolling back obstacles to freer trade and investment. And yet there has probably not been a time in the post-war period when the prospect for further trade and investment liberalisation, one of the surest and quickest ways of harnessing the benefits of a globalising economy, has generated as much public anxiety, not least within those countries that have built much of their prosperity on a liberal trade and investment order.

Liberalisation efforts and public anxiety ...

Communicating the overall benefits of market openness has admittedly never been easy. While market liberalisation generates gains in the aggregate, such net benefits are neither distributed evenly over time nor across various groups of workers, firms, regions or countries. Alongside changing technologies and reforms in domestic regulatory practices to which they are often closely tied, trade and investment liberalisation can entail real economic and social dislocation. The incidence, importance and duration of such disruption matter greatly, particularly as it is typically more concentrated and up-front, while benefits are more diffuse and can take longer to materialise. Experience shows, however, that the economy-wide benefits of open markets are likely to be held back so long as the costs of adjusting to competition have not been borne. So too may the benefits of market openness be held back by inadequate or poorly designed structural adjustment policies. The challenge for policy-makers is thus to take account of distributional issues and transitional costs by designing policies aimed at easing adjustment to changing economic

... over the consequences of greater market openness

circumstances. A central message of this study, however, is that the price of trying to *suppress* these changes would be to so reduce overall economic growth that the balance of effects would be socially regressive.

Calls to slow down the pace of market liberalisation or even to reverse the liberal framework of policies which emerged after World War II are being made with increasing frequency. The fact that such calls can find a ready audience shows that the public concerns are real. It is important that such concerns be acknowledged and addressed. At the same time, it would be an enormous mistake to retreat from core policies that have delivered – and will continue to deliver – prosperity for our citizens. But it cannot be simply taken for granted that the reasons for this prosperity are readily understood. These reasons have to be explained in a forthright yet objective way. This means that there is an urgent need for more balanced and informed policy debates, within and outside the OECD area, on the implications of a sustained commitment to market openness. The case for open trade and investment is as robust today as when Adam Smith or David Ricardo first formulated it two centuries ago. Indeed, it is even stronger in today's globalising environment. By reducing the constraints of time and space, technology and greater economic linkages among countries at all levels of development allow the gains from trade and investment liberalisation to reach more people around the world than ever before. A pre-condition for realising these gains, however, is that the pursuit of liberalisation enjoys broader public support

Liberalisation must enjoy broader political support

To a considerable degree, the erosion of support for liberalisation in certain quarters in recent years reflects a communication deficit. It is vital to recall, therefore, what trade and investment liberalisation can and cannot do, or

be held responsible for; in documenting the tangible benefits of market openness; in pointing out the very real costs of protectionism for consumers' pockets; and, especially, in countering the arguments of those who would want to slow or reverse the trend toward greater market integration.

Communicating the benefits of market openness is key

The reluctance of some in industrialised countries to support calls for further trade and investment liberalisation often forms part of a broader reaction and resistance to the far-reaching changes – in technology, firm conduct, work patterns, employment prospects, income distribution, intensified competitive conditions or the role of government – that are commonly attributed to the process of globalisation.[3] The economic and social impacts of population ageing and the concerns it is evoking over the ability of governments to finance health care and pension benefits add to the sense of collective insecurity. And insecurity, in turn, breeds further resistance to change. Rising levels of immigration in some countries also generate worries over whether there will be sufficient jobs for all who want them. To some extent, these concerns reflect a sense that globalisation is eroding the capacity for self-government, thereby encroaching on domestic politics and sovereign choices. Fears that trade and investment liberalisation rhyme with fewer and lower-paying jobs, unsafe food, or environmental degradation are now commonplace.

More needs to be done also to put matters into a proper context. There is a need to better inform the public of the close links that bind trade and investment liberalisation to the broad range of policies– education, training, taxation, pension reform, the portability of health care benefits – aimed at helping citizens

Liberalisation is part of a bigger picture

and communities take advantage of and adjust to technology-driven structural transformations whose pace and depth are unprecedented. This underlines the importance of presenting market liberalisation not as some abstract end in itself but as an important component of a coherent set of policies aimed at bringing about durable improvements in living standards.

It is not surprising that much of the adverse reaction to globalisation and its alleged dislocating effects should tend to crystallise on efforts at liberalising trade and investment. The proliferation of recent liberalisation initiatives, and the tendency for negotiations to treat a growing range of "behind-the-border" domestic regulatory issues such as safety standards for food, or local content requirements, have given trade and investment liberalisation negotiations an immediacy and proximity that were largely absent from earlier efforts at removing border barriers to manufactured goods alone. Public concern is likewise aroused by the absence or perceived shortcomings, most notably in terms of legal enforceability, of governance regimes in a number of areas – such as the environment or labour standards – that are increasingly intertwined with trade and investment as globalisation unfolds.

In this age of mass communication, these factors have noticeably raised public awareness of trade and investment rule-making, a process many – including influential people in business, politics and civil society – have come to regard as embodying all that is to be feared from globalisation: an alleged loss of political, economic or regulatory sovereignty and heightened pressures for "downward" movement in social, environmental and product standards, the so-called "race to the bottom".

A central aim of this study is to address these genuine concerns; to determine the degree to which actual experience and serious empirical work supports them and to ask counterfactually whether and how policies that would reverse the trend towards greater market integration are likely to resolve the problems perceived to arise from trade and investment liberalisation. The challenge is how best to state the positive case for open markets. To this end, the study recalls the various channels through which open markets deliver considerable gains to societies and their citizens, and how this process actually brings durable benefits to the citizens and countries that pursue liberalisation.

Stating the positive case for open markets

The paper is structured as follows.

- Chapter 2 describes the close links between market liberalisation and growing economic integration and prosperity in the post-war period.

- Chapter 3 states the case for open markets, emphasising both the key benefits of trade and investment liberalisation and the equally tangible pocketbook costs of protectionism, also covered in Appendix A.

- Chapter 4 addresses a number of specific concerns that are raised about market openness.

- Chapters 5 to 7 focus in turn on the distributional, environmental and sovereignty-related concerns that tend to arise in discussions of trade and investment liberalisation.

- Chapter 8 concludes by offering a few thoughts on how to further promote greater public understanding of the benefits flowing from a sustained commitment to open markets.

NOTES

1. See OECD (1997m).

2. The significant economic turmoil which erupted in a number of Asian countries while this study was in its final stages of preparation has provoked a lively debate on its potential impact within the region and beyond. Though it is still difficult to forecast the consequences of the Asian crisis with any precision, it is obvious that confidence in the continuous smooth development of world-wide economic integration has been shaken somewhat. This will no doubt feed some of the anxieties referred to in this study, at least until the required adjustments to domestic economic and regulatory policies in those Asian countries are implemented and begin to prove their effectiveness. Still, it is important to observe that the recent financial turmoil in certain Asian economies is widely seen as arising from the interaction of a number of financial and structural weaknesses, among which the misallocation of resources arising from directed lending, favouritism, over-leveraged corporate balance sheets, non-performing loans by banks, inadequate systems of prudential supervision, rising current account deficits (often associated with non-productive domestic investments), currency appreciation, herd behaviour on the part of foreign portfolio investors, and moral hazard problems arising from implicit government guarantees on external borrowing. The crisis cannot, however, be ascribed to the degree of trade and FDI liberalisation achieved in the countries concerned. On the contrary, had liberalisation been accompanied - and supported - by greater transparency, predictability and competition, notably in the financial sector, the likelihood of the crisis might have been lessened and its effects mitigated. A fuller depiction of the links between banking sector liberalisation and financial crises is provided in Appendix B to the study.

3. See Sachs (1998).

TRADE AND INVESTMENT LEAD THE WAY TO MARKET INTEGRATION

More workers in more firms in more countries derive their livelihood from cross-border trade and investment activity than ever before. So trade and investment liberalisation, and the design of policies to underpin their expansion and to ensure that the gains from liberalisation are maximised (while any adverse affects are properly addressed), are of greater importance to citizens and workers today than they have been throughout the post-war period.

Trade and investment are more important than ever

Trade and investment have become major engines of growth in developed and developing countries alike. The volume of world merchandise trade is today about sixteen times what it was in 1950, a period during which the value of world output increased by a factor of 5.5 (see Figure 2.1). The period since 1950 saw a near doubling, from 8 to 15 per cent, of the ratio of world merchandise exports to global production. Most remarkable has been the accelerating pace of trade-led integration: during 1985-96, the ratio of trade to world GDP rose three times faster than in the preceding decade, and nearly twice as fast as in the 1960s. Services trade has also grown at a rapid pace, becoming one of the fastest growing components of world trade since the mid 1980s. These facts underscore an important point that, far from being a zero-sum game, increased trade and investment and the greater prosperity it brings, are a win-win proposition.

If continuing growth in world trade levels is the most obvious indicator of expanding integration, increases in flows of foreign direct investment (FDI) suggest even more the deepening of such integration. Outflows of FDI experienced a twenty-five-fold rise – from $14 billion to $350 billion – during the last quarter century (see Figure 2.2). With some $6.5 trillion in global sales in 1996 – the value of goods and services produced by the 280,000 foreign affiliates of the world's 44,000 parent firms – international production outweighs exports as the dominant mode of servicing foreign markets. The growth of global sales has exceeded that of exports by a factor of 1.2 to 1.3 since 1987. These trends have combined to make foreign direct investment the most dynamic integrating force in the world economy.[1]

The integrating role of investment

While the main investment focus of this study lies with foreign direct investment, which can be defined as ownership of assets in one country by residents of another for purposes of controlling the use of those assets, other forms of investment and capital flows, notably portfolio investment and bank loans, have also experienced significant growth and are often on people's minds when discussing globalisation-related issues.[2] Despite the Asian financial crisis which shook capital markets in the latter part of 1997, activity on the international financial markets last year reached a level of nearly $1.8 trillion, a 10 per cent increase from 1996, making 1997 the fourth consecutive record year. Flows of portfolio and related investment have more than doubled since 1993, and represented more than five times the level of world FDI flows in 1996.[3] (See Box 2.1 for a discussion of some of the concerns relating to the liberalisation of portfolio investment.)

Information and technology flows represent the third major force driving market integration. During the past two decades there has been an explosion in the absolute amount of knowledge and technology – both of which are embedded in and diffused through trade and investment flows – but, more importantly, in their availability and usefulness to a growing share of the world's population. This period has also seen the marked internationalisation of the research and development (R&D)

activities of multinational enterprises, which have greatly enhanced cross-border technology flows, as well as the increased importance of international sourcing in the diffusion of technology. As OECD economies become increasingly knowledge-based, production methods, consumption patterns, and the interaction between manufacturing and services activities are all changing under the influence of rapid technological development. Nowhere is this more spectacular than in the area of information technology.[4] At both the national and international levels, well functioning systems of innovation and technology diffusion are proving essential to realising productivity gains, economic growth, environmental improvements, job creation and higher living standards[5].

The benefits of trade and investment liberalisation are not all about large or global companies. The growing integration of manufacturing and services activities, and the lowered transaction and information costs associated with open markets, relate to small-

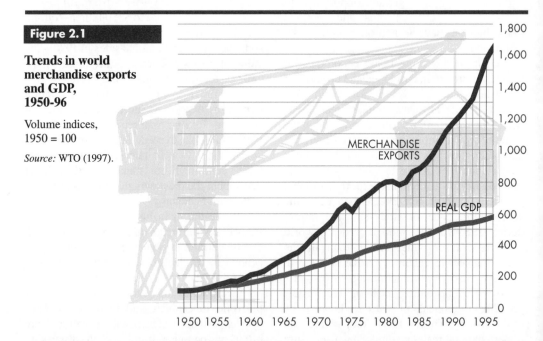

Figure 2.1

Trends in world merchandise exports and GDP, 1950-96

Volume indices, 1950 = 100

Source: WTO (1997).

Box 2.1

Liberalisation and international portfolio investment

International capital flows involve primarily debt and equity. When an investor acquires shares in a foreign enterprise for the purpose of having an effective voice in its management or when both creditor and foreign borrower belong to the same multinational enterprise (MNE), the flows are considered as foreign direct investment (FDI). When there is no controlling ownership link, the capital flow is usually considered as portfolio investment. The association of FDI with long-term investment and portfolio flows with short-term and more speculative investment does not reflect the complexity of modern, sophisticated capital markets. Many institutional investors, for example, might hold long-term stakes in foreign companies in which they exert no managerial control.

Whether portfolio or direct, international investment improves global resource allocation by directing world savings to where they are most productive, by allowing recipient countries to maintain stable levels of investment and consumption in spite of fluctuations in their income, and by sending important signals to host countries concerning the sustainability of their policies. Properly designed liberalisation programmes should also be conceived as an integral part of the structural reform process in emerging market economies where, as clearly apparent from the recent financial market turmoil, government intrusion in direct corporate financing from abroad and lack of transparency in foreign investment regimes discourages necessary progress in corporate governance and banking safety and soundness.

In contrast to FDI, portfolio flows are often criticised for their volatility. It is clear that heavy reliance on external financing – particularly short-term portfolio investment – makes the recipient country vulnerable to changes in international market conditions and shifts in foreign investors' sentiment. It may also involve an element of foreign exchange risk, which renders external borrowing riskier than domestic-based finance and makes decisions by foreign investors very much dependent on exchange rate expectations. However, foreign investors are not inherently more prone to speculation or subject to panic than national investors. Like any investors, they look for the best returns for any given level of risk and liquidate their investments when economic conditions deteriorate. In fact, in recent financial crises, possibly due to better access to information, domestic investors may have reacted even more promptly to signs of deterioration, and contributed more to capital flight, than foreign investors.[8]

When confronted with "capital inflow" problems, countries have sometimes restricted foreign investment. These capital controls tend to create important inefficiencies and to lose their effectiveness in the longer run. They cannot substitute for consistent macroeconomic policies and necessary structural, regulatory, and institutional reforms. On the contrary, capital controls may give the authorities a false sense of security and distract them from their essential task of maintaining sound fiscal and monetary policies and a realistic exchange rate and of pursuing reforms over the medium term.

Experience in OECD countries has shown that, rather than re-imposing capital controls, the most appropriate alternative for a country to prevent financial market instability and to redress a loss of confidence of foreign investors is to encourage long-term foreign investment through credible commitments to investment protection and liberalisation, sound macro-economic policies, strong prudential supervision and transparency.[9]

Table 2.1

Small and Medium-sized enterprises (SMEs) in world trade (latest year available)

Country	Share of SMEs exports (as of total exports)	Percentage of exporting SMEs	N° of Employees	Notes
Australia	15*	5-10*	0-100	
Canada	9	14	5-200	based on data from Quebec
Denmark	46*	n.a.	<500	
France	26*	n.a.	20-499	
Ireland	n.a.	25	<500	
Italy	53		<500	
		68	51-100	
		80	101-300	
		83	301-500	
Japan	13.5	n.a.	<300	(direct)
	30-35		51-100	(indirect)
Korea	40	n.a.	<300	
Netherlands	26		<100	(direct and indirect)
		17	0-9	
		43	10-99	
		67	100+	
Spain	n.a.	18	<20	
		50	51-100	
		70	101-200	
Sweden	36	n.a.	<200	
Switzerland	40	n.a.	<500	
United Kingdom	n.a.	16-20	<500	
United States	11*	12*	<500	
Indonesia	10	n.a.	<100	
Chinese Taipei	56	n.a.	<100	
Thailand	10	n.a.	<100	
Malaysia	15	n.a.	<75	
Singapore	16	n.a.	<100	

*Manufacturing   Source: OECD (1997d).

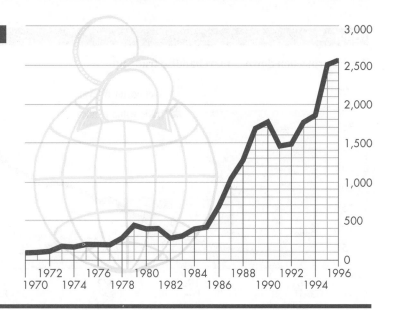

Figure 2.2

Trends in global FDI, 1970-96

Value index, 1970 = 100

Source: UNCTAD (1997).

and medium-sized enterprises (SMEs). As Table 2.1 shows, the potential for smaller firms from developed and developing countries alike to expand in the global marketplace and sustain employment at home is enormous. Within the OECD area, SMEs account for significant shares of total exports: in Italy (53 per cent); Denmark (46 per cent); Korea and Switzerland (40 per cent each); Sweden (36 per cent); France and the Netherlands (26 per cent each). Also noteworthy is the fact that SMEs are in many countries actively engaged in cross-border activity. Data compiled by the US Department of Commerce for the United States indicated that small firms (i.e. with less than 500 employees) represented 95.7 per cent of firms exporting merchandise in 1992.[6] The comparable figure for Canada was 97 per cent in 1995.[7]

These trends reflect the enormous strides made during the past five decades in dismantling the barriers to trade and investment that were erected prior to and since World War II (see Figure 2.3). Fuelled by the idea that markets are supportive of enhanced freedom of individual and collective choice, an overwhelming majority of countries have today come to recognise the critical importance of market-oriented policies and open trade and investment for driving economic growth and improving the material well-being of citizens.

Liberalisation means a bigger economic pie ...

The great bulk of the world's population today lives in economies in which markets are (or are quickly becoming) the prime mechanism for allocating resources. Accordingly, the size of the world's economic pie and the opportunities it affords to firms and consumers alike have increased significantly over the last decade.

Broad acceptance of the merits of market-oriented policies has contributed to a period of sustained growth and rising prosperity.

... and sustains growth

The analogy of a trade and investment-driven tide lifting all boats is apt. Indeed, the remarkable success of the postwar push for an orderly, rules-based reduction of barriers to international commerce is not altogether removed from the fact that poverty has declined significantly during the past five decades – more, in fact, than in the previous five centuries according to the United Nations'

Figure 2.3

Border protection down ... merchandise trade up

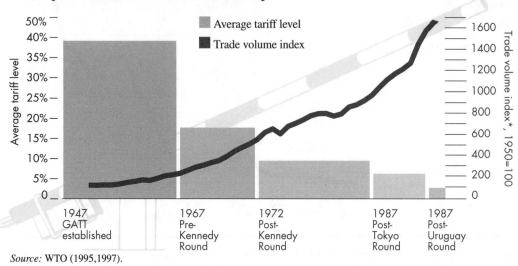

Source: WTO (1995,1997).

latest Human Development Report. While it remains true – and utterly unacceptable – that 1.5 billion people still live in poverty today, it is equally true the rise in living standards associated with a more liberal trading order has played some part in lifting an estimated 3 billion people out of poverty during the post-war period (see Box 2.2). There can similarly be little doubt that the demonstration effect of the growing economic prosperity of countries that took advantage of global trade and investment liberalisation – as well as more market-oriented policies generally – played some part in hastening the end of the Cold War. It also helps explain why so many countries in today's world are increasingly pursuing market-friendly policies.

Market integration fostered by trade and investment has led to deeper forms of economic interdependence among nations – deeper, but also more democratic, as a growing number of developing and former centrally-planned economies have become more closely tied into the global economy. While trade and investment linkages between OECD eco-

nomies remain pre-dominant, the ties that bind developed and developing countries are closer today than ever before.

Market integration hastens greater economic interdependence between the developed and developing world

OECD countries now depend on developing countries for a quarter of their export sales – a forty per cent jump over the level prevailing two decades ago, a fifth of their primary commodity imports, and almost half of their petroleum consumption. Developing country markets now take in one third of global foreign direct investment, with inflows to these countries seventeen times higher in 1996 than a decade earlier.

Developing countries, for their part, rely on OECD countries for more than 60 per cent of their trade and 47 per cent of their primary commodity imports. Inflows of FDI, the bulk of which originates in OECD countries, rank amongst the most important sources of external funding in the developing world, accounting for some 40 per cent of net long-term flows. Trade and investment ties *between* developing countries are also on the rise: they sold more than a third of their exports to each other in 1996, compared with less than a quarter a decade ago. Firms from developing countries are now investing more actively abroad, usually in other developing countries within the same region but also in OECD markets.[11] Developing countries have also greatly diversified their trade linkages both with one another and with OECD countries. Between 1950 and 1980, the share of manufactured products in the total exports of developing countries hovered between 30 and 40 per cent. Beginning in 1981, this hitherto flat trend moved sharply upward, reaching a remarkable 84 per cent in 1996.

Such striking structural shifts in the extent and depth of countries' participation in international trade and investment reflect a sea change in attitudes and policy approaches, marked by the abandonment of inward-looking policies based on protection and import substitution in favour of an outward orientation. While the trend has proceeded at differing speeds at different times in various settings, its world-wide dimension is unmistakable. Since the launching of the Uruguay Round in 1986, over sixty developing nations have unilaterally lowered their barriers to imports, often in the context of a far-reaching reorientation of domestic economic policies. More and more countries, developed and developing, are liberalising imports, promoting exports, welcoming foreign investment, and loosening restrictions on capital flows. Such a strategy has provided the bedrock of industrialised countries' rising prosperity, and propelled a number of emerging economies into the front ranks of trading nations and recipients of foreign investment.

A sea change in attitudes to trade and investment

Box 2.2

Trade and investment liberalisation and poverty reduction in the developing world: contrasted experiences

The record of growth and poverty reduction achieved by the developing countries that oriented their economies towards dynamic participation in world trade, investment and technology flows stands as one of the most remarkable episodes in the history of economic development, even with much unfinished business and a vulnerability to setbacks as highlighted recently in the Asian financial crisis. Living standards have improved dramatically in outward-oriented countries, notably in Asia, ranging from the East Asian "tigers" (Korea; Chinese Taipei, Singapore; Hong Kong, China) to three emerging Southeast Asian economies of Malaysia, Thailand and Indonesia. In 1975, six out of ten Asians lived in absolute poverty (defined as less than $1 of income a day), a plight that afflicts two out of ten Asians today. Equally compelling in this regard is the case of China which, with a population of 1.2 billion, managed to bring down the number of its people living in poverty from 60 per cent at the onset of economic reforms in 1978 to 27 per cent in 1994. Some of the poorest countries in the region such as India, Sri Lanka and Vietnam may also get onto a faster track to economic growth by putting in place the policies that facilitate linkages to global markets for goods, capital and services.

In sharp contrast, the poverty reduction record has been disappointing and even negative in those countries, whether relatively advanced or relatively poor, that pursued economic policies unfriendly to market forces and international trade and investment. Studies comparing the thirty-year performance of selected African countries (Nigeria, Côte d'Ivoire and Tanzania) with three Southeast Asian economies, Malaysia, Thailand and Indonesia, show how these two groups of countries, which started out with similar economic structures and income

(continued on following page)

Box 2.2 (continued)

levels in the 1960s, fared differently in growth, poverty reduction and income distribution depending in large measure on their policy orientation.[10]

These studies conclude that the two key factors which contributed to the success of South-East Asian economies were the encouragement given to the private sector and the strong emphasis placed on export development. A range of policies were implemented to achieve these objectives, including a focus on exchange rate adjustments, measures to lift performance standards in agriculture and industry and massive investments in education.

It is clear that the success stories achieved through trade-led integration involved much more than the opening of markets and a welcoming environment for international investment. Political leadership is also critical to reforming major areas of economic dysfunction, establishing effective governance systems under the rule of law and managing the social transitions that accompany the liberalisation process.

The financial crises in a number of Asian countries serve only to underline that these challenges are ever present. It is all the more evident that sustained political leadership and attention to the soundness of financial, regulatory and corporate structures and behaviour are essential. The events in Asia are a useful reminder of the differences that exist between a narrower outward trade orientation and comprehensively liberal trade and investment regimes. These are not necessarily the same thing, and certain Asian economies that have been export-oriented are experiencing problems in part at least because significant work remains to be done to open key sectors more fully to foreign competition, notably in the financial area.

The failure to make human development and economic efficiency the key national priorities contributed greatly to Africa's lagging development. The greater commitment of a new generation of African leaders to a policy reform agenda based on a trade and FDI-led integration lends hope that stronger links with the world economy will boost economic growth and provide the highway to poverty reduction. For OECD countries too, the stakes are high. An African continent failing to make real progress can generate crises with highly negative humanitarian and economic spillovers in areas such as food security, resource depletion, conflict, crime, migration, drugs and financial problems, impacting on world security and welfare. Successful integration in the world economy, on the other hand, could turn Africa into an important source of trade and investment creation and a partner in confronting the challenges of sustainable development in the twenty-first century.

Equally remarkable is how governments have stayed the course of market-led reforms – indeed, even accelerated them – when confronted with occasional and potentially significant macro-economic difficulties. For example, in the wake of the country's 1994 currency crisis, the government of Mexico deepened its commitment to trade and investment liberalisation under the North American Free Trade Agreement. And, in December 1997, in the midst of a major disruption in Asian financial markets, a number of emerging economies agreed to far-reaching liberalisation commitments on financial services within the framework of the World Trade Organization (WTO). The fact that Mexico recovered from its crisis in a relatively short period of time provides confirmation of the fact that continued liberalisation and economic progress can go hand-in-hand.

Three developments illustrate the worldwide trend towards greater market openness:

- first, the recent surge in regional trading arrangements (RTAs), itself a response to, and a reflection of, expanding regional trade and investment ties. Between 1990 and 1994, 33 RTAs were notified to the GATT/WTO, a third of all regional deals negotiated since 1948;

- second, the literal explosion in the number of bilateral investment protection agreements – more than 1,600 in all, with some 800 in the 1990s and one *every* two days in 1996 alone! Such growth is the surest sign of an expanding global economic pie and the opportunities it affords to traders and investors; and

- third, the lengthening list of countries – thirty-two at latest count, including China and Russia – seeking admission to the World Trade Organization, thirty-one countries having joined the GATT/WTO since 1986.

Among the reasons for the impressive queue at the WTO's doorstep are the very tangible rewards – in the form of higher living standards –which accrue to countries that take trade and investment liberalisation seriously. (See Appendix C) More open and outward-oriented economies consistently outperform countries with restrictive trade and investment regimes (see Figure 3.1).[12] And adherence to multilaterally-agreed rules has proven time and again as one of the best means of keeping markets open at home and abroad.

More open economies out perform those with more restrictive policies

NOTES

1. The impact of FDI-led integration is illustrated by the growing share of global business that takes place on an intra-firm and intra-industry basis, and the increasing importance of trade in intermediate inputs, a rising proportion of which consists of services.

2. The liberalisation and deregulation of financial markets and the advent of new information technologies, together with the emergence of new financial instruments, have given major impetus to that growth. For example, the value of cross-border assets held by banks more than tripled between 1973 and 1995; average daily turnover in foreign exchange markets have grown from about $200 billion in the mid-1980s to more than $1.2 trillion today, equivalent to approximately 85 per cent of all countries' foreign exchange reserves. Even after allowing for resale, daily foreign exchange transactions amount to well over $600 billion, or about fifty times the daily value of total world-wide trade in merchandise and services. In addition, cross-border transactions in bonds and equities in the major advanced economies reached 100 percent of GDP in 1995, as compared to 10 percent just ten years ago. See BIS (1997) and OECD (1995).

3. See OECD (1998a).

4. Not only is the information technology (IT) sector assuming a central facilitating role in the globalisation of the world economy, it is also a commercial powerhouse in its own right. Trade in IT products, which stood at $626 billion in 1996, grew by 13 percent a year on average during 1990-96, the fastest growth of all major product categories in merchandise trade. Such trade is expected to reach $800 billion by the year 2000. IT's 12.2 percent share of total goods trade places it on par with agriculture, and well ahead of automobile products' 9.2 percent, or of iron and steel, textiles and clothing exports, the *combined* share of which amounted to 8.8 percent of world merchandise trade in 1996. The growing commercial and economy-wide importance of the IT sector lies behind the successful completion of the WTO's landmark Information Technology Agreement in December 1996. The Agreement provides for the elimination of tariffs on a wide range of IT products by the year 2000. See Fliess, B. and Sauvé P. (1998).

5. See Ostry, S., "Technology Issues in the International Trading System", in OECD (1996c) pp. 145-70. See also OECD (1996a) and OECD (1997f).

6. Small firm exporters were especially dominant in the wholesale trade and transportation services industries, making up 99.2 percent of US exporters in 1992, the latest year for which data is available. About 12 per cent of small US manufacturing firms reported exporting activities in that year.

7. See Government of Canada (1997).

8. On the Mexican peso crisis of 1994-95, see IMF (1995). See also Frankel, J.A. and Schmukler, S.L. (1996).

9. See "Financial Sector Liberalisation in Emerging Markets", in *OECD (1997e)*.

10. See OECD (1997g).

11. See for instance UNCTAD (1996a).

12. See also Ng, F. and Yeats, A. (1996).

THE CASE FOR OPEN MARKETS

I. DOCUMENTING THE BENEFITS OF MARKET LIBERALISATION

The case for open markets rests on a few core foundations. One of them is grounded in the strong preference of people the world over for more, rather than less, freedom of choice.

Open markets bring greater freedom of choice, specialisation and exchange

A world with reduced trade or investment is a world with less of that freedom of choice: whether this is over what to buy and to sell and at what price; where to obtain inputs; where and how to invest; or what skills to acquire.

A second core foundation is based on the age-old principle of comparative advantage: countries, like individuals, prosper when they use their resources – natural, human, industrial, financial – to concentrate on what they do well relative to others. The essence of the case for liberal trade and investment is that incomes will be higher, nationally and internationally, if individuals and companies are free to engage in specialisation and exchange. Specialisation allows both businesses and individuals to deploy their relative strengths, abilities and expertise. Freedom of exchange through trade and investment lowers prices, broadens the range of quality goods and services available to firms and consumers, and allows investors to diversify risks, channel resources to where returns are highest and secure access to capital at the lowest possible cost.

In short, open markets allow resources to be used more efficiently and productively. The efficiency benefits of an open trade and investment regime contribute to economic growth and hence rising incomes (see Figure 3.1). By contrast, restrictions on trade and investment, in common with other economic distortions, shift an economy to a less efficient and sustainable mix of investment, production and consumption patterns, thus depressing economic growth prospects and reducing attendant benefits such as job creation and innovation.[1]

Open trade and investment helps firms tap into world markets, increase their sales potential, realise economies of scale and spread the fixed costs of research and development over a wider customer base. Each of these improves profit, which sustains employment and investment. Market openness brings real, direct economic gains to *all* consumers – whether firms or individuals. Firms benefit from better access to competitive sources of materials, components and services. Individuals benefit because lower prices and greater product diversity increase the purchasing power of their wages. Imports can also help dampen inflation by disciplining the price behaviour of domestic producers. And low inflation, in turn, leads to greater returns on savings. Australia's example over the past decade is telling in this regard:

Openness means gains for countries and individuals

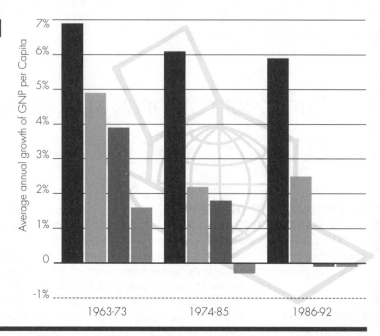

Figure 3.1

**The rewards
of openness:
trade orientation
and living standards
in developing countries**

■ Strongly
outward-oriented

▨ Moderately
outward-oriented

■ Strongly inward-oriented

■ Moderately
inward-oriented

Source: Greenaway *et al* (1989)
and IMF (1997).

tariff reductions alone having put an estimated A$1,000 a year in the pockets of the average Australian family.[2]

Trade and investment liberalisation increases the geographic range of competition, thereby enhancing opportunities to absorb new and more productive processes. Productivity levels tend to be highest in industries that are exposed, through imports, exports and foreign direct investment, to substantial competition from world-class producers.[3] And the higher productivity resulting from such "emulation" effects translates into improved company earnings, which contribute to economic growth and the creation of jobs.

Liberalisation promotes competition, productivity gains and encourages best practice production methods

Exposure to trade and foreign investment also provides powerful incentives to local producers to lift their performance by mini-mising waste, improving production techniques and using research and development to generate innovations that will enhance their products' competitiveness. By encouraging the adoption of best-practice production processes, trade and investment facilitate the transfer of ideas, know-how and technologies across borders.[4] A higher degree of openness allows smaller countries to absorb technologies developed in other countries at a faster rate and thus to grow more rapidly than countries that are less open.[5] From a policy perspective, all of these results reinforce the conclusion that exposure to best practice productivity methods and products through trade and investment liberalisation promotes greater overall efficiency in resource use.[6] A more open domestic market is far from being a handicap. Quite the contrary, it is a source of competitive strength.

The signalling function of free and open trade and investment is just as important for countries as it is for firms or workers, as open and flexible markets help countries adapt to and cushion the effects of shifts in comparative advantage. For OECD countries, market openness encourages the redeployment of highly skilled and educated workforces towards the emerging knowledge-based activities in which they enjoy a strong competitive edge. Keeping OECD markets open to developing country exports is also crucial if the latter are to achieve durable gains in living standards. OECD countries gain in this process, both because the countries concerned sell better quality products to OECD consumers at competitive prices and because OECD countries export higher value-added goods and services. International trade and investment is not a matter where some countries win and others lose. In fact, trade and investment allow *all* countries to achieve greater prosperity (see Box 3.1).

Empirical research shows that exporters are more prone to be "on their competitive toes" than domestic non-exporting and non-import competing firms.[8] This explains why exporting firms typically rank among countries' most prosperous businesses. An important source of that prosperity rests on the higher productivity of workers employed in export-intensive sectors. Higher productivity means higher wages for those workers. It also means more prosperous communities in which exporting firms are located and workers live. Exactly the same picture obtains in the case of foreign direct investment. Indeed, in every single OECD country for which data exists, workers in firms and sectors with high export- and FDI-intensity earn a substantial wage premium and show above-average labour productivity (see Figures 3.2, 3.3 and 3.4). By implication,

Box 3.1

The challenge of adjusting to trade spares no countries

During the past three decades, many poor countries have experienced rapid economic development after adopting liberal economic policies. In manufacturing sectors such as apparel assembly, a "cascading" pattern of growth has accompanied this global movement toward openness. Production has expanded in poorer countries, responding to shifts in various countries' comparative advantage. The shift of garment assembly to poorer countries has reflected its continuing labourintensity: low unit labour costs in poor economies have in many cases been sufficient to offset the potential for automated production in higher-wage countries.[7] The world garment "story" could well be characterised as a continuous search for low-cost production sites by apparel manufacturers.

Such developments recall how the process of trade-induced adjustment applies to countries at all levels of development. Moreover, it illustrates how trends that often lead to calls for import protectionism in developed countries are in fact, salutary from the perspective of development economics: exports of garments and other assembly goods have served as the first rung on the ladder of rapid income growth and skills development for millions of poor workers. It was not that long ago that this applied to workers from OECD countries.

The story of the gains from trade does not end there however. Consumers in developed countries benefit because they can buy garments for themselves and their families more cheaply. Producers also benefit because developing countries moving up the income ladder typically spend their export proceeds by buying more sophisticated manufactured products such as chemicals, computers and machinery from developed countries

communities with large numbers of export-reliant plants or which play host to significant levels of foreign direct investment are more likely to enjoy growing tax bases.

Figures for the US, on which data are most readily available, are particularly telling. Labour productivity in plants producing for export has been 40 per cent higher than in equivalent plants producing only for the home market, and their productivity growth over the 1986-94 period was nearly three times the

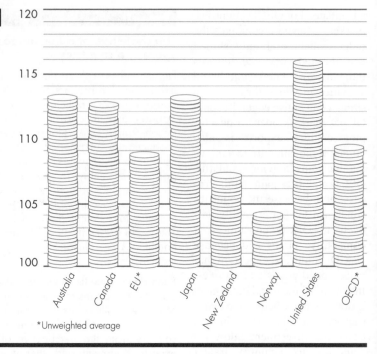

Figure 3.2

The payoff from exports: wages

Earnings of export sectors as a per cent of average manufacturing earnings

Source: OECD (1997*b*).

*Unweighted average

national average.[9] In 1994, the wages of all production and related workers in jobs supported by goods exports were 13 per cent higher than the national average, and the wages of workers in jobs supported directly by those exports were 20 per cent higher.[10] Employment growth in exporting firms has been systematically higher than in comparable non-exporting firms, and export-supported jobs accounted for 31 per cent of the rise in total US employment between 1986 and 1994. People working in high-technology firms have fared even better, the average hourly earnings of workers supported directly by their own exports being an estimated 34 per cent higher than the national average. Figures for FDI-related jobs paint a similar picture: productivity and compensation per employee in foreign-owned establishments is higher than for US-owned establishments. Wages were 26 per cent higher at US subsidiaries than at all private sector business in the country in 1992. Moreover, such higher wages were observed in

all fifty US states.[11] Two reasons explaining such outcomes are that foreign-owned firms are larger than domestic competitors in most cases and are concentrated in high-wage, high-technology US industries.[12]

As the above discussion suggests, the case for open markets is as compelling for investment as it is for trade.[13] This is crucially important given that FDI is today the chief integrating force in the world economy. (See Box 3.2.) More open economies enjoy higher rates of private investment (i.e. including foreign and domestic), which is a major determinant of economic growth. The linkage of openness to growth through investment is particularly strong in the case of foreign direct investment. Countries with more open trade and investment policies attract more FDI, and the growth-enhancing effects of FDI tend to exceed those of domestically financed invest-

The case for liberalising investment is as strong as for trade

ment. One reason is the greater technological spillovers associated with much foreign investment – i.e., innovation, above-average R&D intensity, and skills enhancement.

Recognition of the benefits of *inward* investment is best evidenced by the fierceness of global competition to attract ever greater quantities of FDI.[14] The explosive growth in bilateral investment protection agreements observed of late suggests that the presence of foreign investors is increasingly recognised for what it is — a boon to development (see Box 3.3). Like trade, foreign direct investment acts as a powerful spur to competition and innovation, encouraging domestic firms to reduce costs and enhance their competitiveness. Global production contributes to incomes and employment in the countries in which it takes place.

Figure 3.3

The payoff from FDI : wages

Wages per employee of foreign affiliates in manufacturing

National firms = 100

■ 1985

■ 1994

Source: OECD (1996).

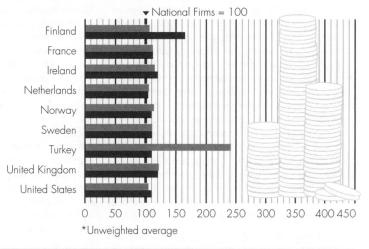

▼ National Firms = 100

Finland
France
Ireland
Netherlands
Norway
Sweden
Turkey
United Kingdom
United States

0 50 100 150 200 250 300 350 400 450

*Unweighted average

Figure 3.4

The payoff from FDI: productivity

Labour productivity of foreign affiliates - 1985 and 1994*

National firms = 100

■ 1985

■ 1994

*Or nearest year.

Source: OECD (1996).

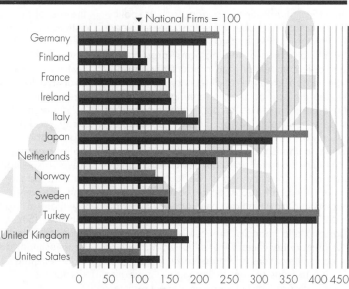

▼ National Firms = 100

Germany
Finland
France
Ireland
Italy
Japan
Netherlands
Norway
Sweden
Turkey
United Kingdom
United States

0 50 100 150 200 250 300 350 400 450

Box 3.2

The world-wide trend towards more liberal investment regimes

The tremendous growth of FDI in recent years has been driven by the interaction of policy reforms and evolving corporate strategies. Technological change has blurred the line between certain sectors, bringing more industries into direct competition. At the same time, more and more firms have sought to capitalise on faster growth abroad than at home. The combined effect has been to push firms beyond their own markets and to bring about a wave of consolidation through cross-border mergers and acquisitions. Underpinning these changes has been the remarkable transformation of policy approaches in many countries, developed and developing. Along with sound macroeconomic management, improved structural policies have been introduced to remove supply-side constraints and to boost productive capacity and economic growth. These policies have involved regulatory reform (including deregulation) privatisation and de-monopolisation on an unprecedented scale, particularly in service-related activities. They have brought major reforms in the financial sector, abolition of exchange controls and more integrated financial markets.

The liberalisation of restrictions on foreign investment has been an important part of countries' market-oriented approach to policy-making, for which they have long been valued. Governments have become more attentive to the beneficial effects of foreign firms' presence on domestic competition and productivity, in addition to job creation and technology transfer. During the past decade, screening mechanisms have been simplified or abolished in favour of simple notification or verification procedures, usually for administrative or statistical purposes, while authorisation requirements have been maintained only for politically sensitive large new transactions or acquisitions. Sectoral restrictions have also been abolished or eased, and new sectors and activities have been opened to private enterprises and foreign participation. The banking and financial services sector has been the primary beneficiary, but other sectors such as telecommunications and broadcasting, partly due to the impetus of new technologies, have also faced a less restrictive foreign investment regime.

Liberalisation has had a "knock-on" effect as reforms in some countries have drawn attention to the restrictions of others and offered evidence of the benefits to be gained from introducing more liberal policies. Regional initiatives – in particular the Single Market initiative and en-largement of the European Economic Community, and the North American Free Trade Agreement (NAFTA) – have also fuelled the process of liberalisation. Globalisation and the emergence of new markets have also encouraged the removal of obstacles to outward direct investment so that domestic firms could take better advantage of growth potential abroad. Virtually all restrictions on the authorisation and financing of outward direct investment from OECD countries have now been removed. Sectoral liberalisation has been accompanied by an increasing recourse to reciprocity requirements, especially in finance, transport and public utilities (gas, electricity, water supply, etc.) The degree of liberalisation achieved so far has been preserved and, in many cases, enhanced, as was the case most recently in the WTO's two landmark agreements on basic telecommunications and financial services.

Liberalisation in OECD countries is echoed in the rest of the world. The UNCTAD secretariat estimates that from 1991 to 1996, only 27 out of almost 600 changes in host country policies towards FDI were in the direction of greater restrictiveness. To facilitate further investment, over 1,600 bilateral investment treaties have been signed, more than half of which during the 1990s alone. Such developments are unambigu-ously good news, signalling as they do a grow-ing number of active trading and investing nations around the world. Such developments have also significantly increased the calls for consolidating the gains from such reforms, as can be seen from the negotiation of a Multilateral Agreement on Investment in the OECD. (See Box 7.2) and by proposals for integrating in future a more comprehensive set of investment disciplines into the WTO along-side existing trade and investment-related disciplines.

In the case of OECD countries, FDI is primarily directed towards high-skilled and high-wage manufacturing and service activities. Foreign investment is actively courted not only because of the direct effects on jobs, tax revenues and economic growth, but also because of the large indirect or "spillover" benefits it generates in host economies: improving the quality of local labour, management and technical know-how that is embodied in superior human and working capital.[15] Improved environmental quality is another potential benefit associated with FDI. OECD firms typically bring their (higher) environmental standards with them when they invest; they also make alliances with local suppliers, encouraging productivity improvements that bring additional spillover benefits, for example by promoting "greener" production methods. There is scant evidence that FDI crowds out domestic investment. Rather, it almost invariably supplements resources that may not be available locally. Moreover, a very high share of value-added generated by foreign-owned companies – up to 90 per cent according to a study recently commissioned by the Government of New Zealand – is reinvested in the host country.[16] By paying above-average wages, buying goods and services, paying taxes, transferring knowledge and technology and re-investing their earnings locally, foreign firms can add considerably more value to host economies than any profits they remit.

The effects of direct investment *outflows* on the source country, particularly on employment, are sometimes still regarded with some disquiet. Most concerns regarding the effects of FDI outflows may arise because investment is viewed statically and without due regard to the spillover effects it generates at home and abroad. In fact, however, domestic firms and their employees generally gain from the freedom of businesses to invest overseas. As with trade, FDI generally creates net benefits for host and source countries alike. As regards more specifically FDI flows directed towards developing countries, around which concerns over the potential for FDI to "export" jobs tend to revolve, it bears recalling that equipping the increasingly skilled work force in such countries with more sophisticated capital will boost workers' productivity and lead to rises both in income (wages) and imports. Good long-term portfolio investments in developing countries will also help the aging workforce of the industrial countries get the most out of their retirement funds.

The possibility of investing abroad broadens the choice of investment options available to firms and can help increase returns while at the same time spreading risks across different markets. These advantages can make the difference between the firm remaining competitive or stagnating. The significance of this for employment is clear. If transferring some of its production capacity abroad helps a firm expand or stay in operation, prompting resources to be channelled toward higher value-added activities at home, then FDI outflows are clearly beneficial for – indeed supportive of – employment as a whole.[17] Moreover, investing abroad may be the only commercially practical option available. This is notably the case of numerous service activities – in finance, professional services or retail trade – where a local presence allowing a firm to tailor its product offerings to local demand is key to competitive survival. Close to 60 per cent of total FDI flows are today directed towards service activities.

FDI outflows help support employment at home ...

All foreign direct investment, abroad and at home, creates secondary flows: exports of machinery and other capital goods, demand for manufactured production inputs, the provision of expertise and specialised services (for instance, finance, accounting,

... while generating complementary export growth

Box 3.3

Foreign direct investment and developing countries

Developing countries increasingly recognise the role that direct investment, both inward and outward, can play in economic development. Foreign investors represent a source of long-term capital, employment in more technologically complex activities and, most importantly, technology and know-how. Multinational enterprises (MNEs), which account for the bulk of FDI, can serve as a conduit for exports from the host country even as they increase competition in domestic markets.

A number of developing countries have been highly successful in pursuing a development strategy based on foreign investment in their economies. In these cases, FDI has been associated with rapid industrialisation and a concomitant expansion of increasingly technologically-sophisticated manufactured exports. The benefits of FDI usually manifest themselves in the host country's trade performance. Initially, inward investment influences the pattern of trade and the type of goods and services that are exported. Most of these export changes are brought about directly through the activities of foreign firms. In the longer term, through transfers of technology and linkages with the local economy, the influence of FDI also shows up in the growing competitiveness of local firms in world markets, including small- and medium-sized enterprises (see Table 2.1).

The contribution of foreign investors to host country development is not solely a function of exports. Technology transfers result in improved productivity which ultimately promotes economic growth. A recent study of 69 developing countries found that FDI not only stimulates economic growth but has a larger impact than investment by domestic firms.[18] In this study, FDI is seen as contributing to growth through two channels: first, by adding to the stock of capital in the host country; second, by being more productive than domestic investment. Rather than crowding out domestic investment, FDI has been found to stimulate such investment. The ultimate effects on growth depend importantly on human resource considerations in host countries, with the greatest benefits accruing to those countries with the highest educational attainment.

As was observed in industrial economies, foreign affiliates operating in developing countries pay higher wages, or total labour compensation, than locally-owned firms. A comparison of foreign manufacturing affiliates with locally owned firms in Côte d'Ivoire, Morocco and Venezuela shows that, in every industry in which the difference was statistically significant, foreign affiliates paid higher wages. Ratios of MNE wages to local firm wage levels were: Morocco, 1.9; Côte d'Ivoire, 1.5; and Venezuela, 1.5. Similar findings are reported for a number of economies in Asia in the manufacturing sector, with wage differentials in Hong Kong, China and Singapore estimated at 21 percent and 38 percent respectively. Data for Thailand in 1990 suggest that wages, average labour productivity (i.e., value-added per employee) and capital intensity (i.e., total assets per employee) were, on average, higher in foreign affiliates of MNEs than in local firms.[19]

Firms from developing countries are also starting to become major outward investors in their own right. Hong Kong, China, Chinese Taipei, Singapore and China have ranked among the top 20 source countries for FDI during the 1990s. Many of these investments flow to other developing countries and involve activities in which the home country no longer enjoys a comparative advantage. But an increasing share also represents investments in the service sector, where developing country firms are becoming increasingly competitive.

As with private sector investment more generally, the benefits from FDI are enhanced in an environment characterised by an open trade and investment regime, an active competition policy, macroeconomic stability, privatisation, regulatory reform, and flexible labour markets. In such environments, FDI can play a key role in improving the capacity of the host country to respond to the opportunities offered by global economic integration, a goal increasingly recognised as one of the key aims of any development strategy.

software design, advanced communications, consulting engineering) which, evidence shows, are usually supplied by the source country.[20] Recent work on a sample of fourteen OECD countries attests to the significance of these linkages and their effect on home country income and employment: each dollar of outward FDI is associated with $2 of *additional* exports and with a bilateral trade *surplus* of $1.7 dollars. These results make it clear that, without outward FDI, OECD country exports would actually be smaller.[21] Thus, outward FDI in fact reinforces the competitiveness of the investor.

The economy-wide benefits of trade and investment liberalisation are particularly important in the case of services. This is so not only because economies, developed and developing, derive the bulk of income and employment growth in the sector but also because of the key infrastructural role that many key service sectors assume. Many modern service sectors, such as telecommunications, finance, professional services and transport, not only provide final consumer products, but basic production inputs for a wide variety of user industries (both goods- and services-producing). Large service sectors have also long been heavily regulated. Both the above characteristics imply that efficiency-enhancing reforms, including regulatory and institutional changes, are likely to promote the competitiveness of many downstream activities while improving overall economic performance. Not surprisingly, empirical evidence suggests that early liberalisation can contribute substantially to a country's locational attractiveness for new investment.[22]

A further dimension of services trade and investment liberalisation that bears emphasising is that the adjustment associated with greater market openness is generally smoother in many service sectors than in some more traditional areas of goods. This is so for two reasons. First, adjustment in service industries such as banking or telecommunications often occur within a dynamic sectoral environment, where expanding segments and firms can more readily absorb workers from shrinking sectors. Second, owing to a lower degree of sector-specific professional specialisation, service sector employees tend to display greater overall labour market mobility.[23]

II. COUNTING THE COSTS OF PROTECTIONISM

Liberalisation, of course, can be disruptive. Countries, firms and workers can be hurt by their competitors' improvements in efficiency. Despite the fact that open trade and investment produces overall gains, some segments of society experience adjustment pains and income losses when markets are opened (or even when domestic reforms are undertaken). This explains why periodic calls are made to protect industries and workers against cheap imports by maintaining or even raising tariffs, imposing quotas or resorting to various non-tariff barriers. Societies typically pay a high price for heeding such calls.

The negative effects of protectionism, whether on individual countries or the world economy, are well documented.[24] Barriers to trade or investment raise the prices of both imports and domestic products, restrict consumer choice and usually lower quality by easing competitive pressure. Protectionism fragments markets, limiting the ability (and reducing the incentive) of firms in the exporting country to lower production costs from specialisation and access to cheaper inputs. By raising prices, higher trade or investment barriers act like a tax hike. Conversely, trade liberalisation is, in effect, a tax cut (see Appendix C). Seen this way, the Uruguay Round outcome can be viewed as a global tax cut of over $200 billion per annum. More recently, the WTO's landmark Information Technology Agreement (ITA), which was reached in December 1996 and calls for the complete removal of tariffs on an

Protectionism operates like a tax hike

Box 3.4

The costs of agricultural protection[25]

Trade in agricultural products takes place against a background of high levels of support to agricultural producers which substantially distort trade flows and generate large economic inefficiencies. In 1997, the so-called "producer subsidy equivalent" (PSE), a measure of the value of monetary transfers to farmers resulting from agricultural policies, averaged 35 per cent of the value of production in the OECD countries, ranging from 3 per cent in New Zealand to 76 per cent in Switzerland. Protection levels differ significantly across commodities, with rice, milk and sugar receiving the highest levels of support A perhaps even better measure of protection than the PSE is the so-called "consumer nominal assistance coefficient" (NAC), which compares world market prices and domestic prices of agricultural

products. When the world price is the same as the domestic price, the NAC equals 1.0. While the average NAC has come down in recent years, from 1.61 in 1986-88 to 1.32 in 1997, consumers in most OECD countries still pay a significant premium over world prices for their food ranging up to, e.g., two and a half times the world price.

Estimates of the static welfare costs of agricultural protection are usually put at 1 to 3 per cent of national income. Assistance in the form of subsidies is, moreover, a burden on public finances. The benefits of trade and investment-distorting interventions usually go to the politically influential, improving the welfare of rent-seeking interest groups at the expense of the general public. What is more, interventions are prone to lead to serious conflict with trading partners.

Consumer Nominal Assistance Coefficients (NACs)

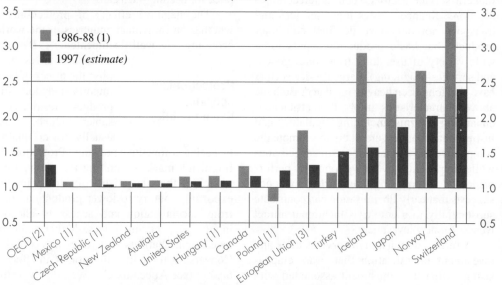

Notes: Countries are ranked according to 1997 levels. NACs lower than one imply that domestic prices are below world prices.
1. For the Czech Republic, Hungary, Mexico and Poland, the first bar refers to the 1989-91 average.
2. Austria, Finland and Sweden are included in the OECD average for the 1986-88 period and in the EU for 1996 and 1997.
   The Czech Republic, Hungary, Mexico, Poland and Korea are not included in the OECD average.
3. European Union = EU-12 for 1986-88; = EU-15 for 1996 and 1997, including the ex-GDR.
Source: OECD Secretariat, 1998.

Table 3.1

Comparing the aggregate costs of protectionism

		United States	Japan	Korea	European Union
	Year	1994	1989	1990	1990
Number of industries surveyed		21	47	49	20
Consumer cost					
billions of dollars		70	74-110	12-13	67-100
share of GDP		1.2	2.6-3.8	3.8-4.3	1.1-1.6
Average tariff equivalent (per cent)		35	180	170	40
Jobs "saved"		190,000	180,000	174,000-405,000	1,500,000
Share of total employment		0.2	0.3	0.9-2.0	1.1
Cost per job saved (dollars)		170,000	600,000	33,000-67,000	70,000

Source: Hufbauer, G. C. (1996).

estimated 92.3 per cent of world trade in IT products over a four-year period starting in 1998, offers a useful reminder of how trade liberalisation can deliver benefits similar to those of a tax cut. The direct and indirect gains accruing annually from the ITA have been estimated at some $50 billion, a *de facto* tax break beneficiaries can now hope to channel to more productive uses.

What is more, because the tax that protection amounts to tends in most OECD countries to be stiffest in the case of food, clothing and footwear, its impact is actually regressive, hitting lower-paid workers and poorer consumers who spend proportionately more of their income on these products. For example, one study found that while a Canadian family belonging to the highest income group earned six times more than a family in the lowest category, the costs borne by the former group due to protection on clothing (tariffs and quotas) were only about twice as high.[26] This is typically the case in

such sectors and should be borne particularly in mind when assessing the effects of overall levels of protection depicted in Box 3.4.

Imposing trade or capital restrictions to prevent some workers from being disadvantaged by greater competition will only make the domestic economic pie smaller, lowering welfare for all workers in the long-run. Trade restrictions protect the domestic market at a high cost to consumers (see Appendix A for an illustrative list of examples of the costs of protectionism). For instance, a recent report by the WTO Secretariat found that "voluntary" export restraints by Japan on automobiles shipped to the European Union (EU) raised the price of Japanese cars to EU consumers by 33 per cent; and that protection against imports of textiles and clothing costs an annual US$310 to every household in the United States and US$220 to

Protectionism shrinks the domestic economy

every Canadian household.[27] Table 3.1 summarises the results of recent research on the aggregate costs of protectionism in a number of major trading nations. Such studies point to the very real welfare losses accruing from restrictive trade measures – accounting for as much as 4 per cent of Korea's total output in 1990, and the considerable resources devoted to maintaining production and employment in protected sectors. Invariably, the average cost to consumers for every job "saved" through protectionism far exceeds average wages, using up resources that could be more usefully spent on job re-training or income support for displaced workers.

Protectionism rarely, if ever, tackles the underlying policy requirement for adjustment, efficiency gains and competitiveness. It encourages firms to engage in costly and wasteful lobbying and dampens competitive pressures, thus encouraging inefficiency and even greater dependence on protection. Once in place, moreover, protectionism is difficult to dismantle, as powerful interest groups mobilise to support it. And protectionism opens the way for retaliation, which both frustrates the original goal of the policy and escalates its costs.

Tariffs or other restrictive measures can protect jobs, but only in the short term. They cannot be counted on to provide longer-term job security. Tariff protection has little long-term positive impact on employment trends, since experience shows that employment tends to fall in highly protected industries, even during periods of high and increasing protectionism. All in all, protectionism imposes costs on the wider economy that far outweigh the gains to those it seeks to assist. Australia provides a case in point, where employment in the textiles, clothing, footwear and motor vehicle industries has fallen steadily over the last twenty-five years even during periods of rising tariffs. In most instances, the long-term fall in employment is deemed to reflect technological changes and underlying market trends, not trade or investment liberalisation.[28]

Trade restrictions impose too high a cost

As Chapter 5 will show, ensuring that a commitment to open trade and investment remains politically acceptable requires policies that ease the plight of those in the front line of adjustment. Policies for those hurt by change are indeed essential so that trade and investment can deliver higher incomes for all, and protectionism can be defeated. Public policies that encourage an upgrading of skills through education and training, and support mobility so as to reduce the cost of moving into new jobs or communities are clearly to be preferred over policies that postpone the day of reckoning.

NOTES

1. The empirical literature on trade and growth confirms and underscores the theoretical case for open trade and investment policies. Several studies documenting the experience of countries having undergone trade liberalisation programmes point to a positive relation between trade liberalisation and growth. Evidence is also mounting that sectoral efficiency levels and/or growth are linked to the degree of international competition. Tariff levels have been found systematically to depress productivity levels and growth in manufacturing sectors, and so-called "efficiency frontier" studies have identified openness as an important determinant of sectoral productivity levels across countries. Studies on services sectors, such as transportation, telecommunications, finance and distribution, also conclude that some of the vast differences in cross-country productivity levels are related to the degree of foreign competition via trade and, especially, foreign direct investment. For a careful review of this literature, see Edwards, S. (1993). See also Pilat, D. (1996); Caves, R. *et al.* (1992), and Baily, M.N. (1993).

2. See Commonwealth of Australia (1997).

3. See Baily, M.N. and Gersbach, H. (1995).

4. See Baily, M.N. (1993), *op.cit.*

5. Including the possibility of making more rapid improvements in local environmental conditions than would otherwise be possible.

6. See US International Trade Commission (1997). See also Pilat, D. (1996), *op.cit.*

7. Despite this general trend, some OECD countries have remained competitive in certain areas of garment production, particularly where productivity improvements have allowed for continued production (albeit often at lower levels of employment) or where production serves highly specialised or customised market segments, such as high fashion (See Box 5.1.).

8. See Richardson, J.D. and Rindal K. (1996) and Bernard, A.B. and Jensen, J.B. (1997).

9. See Richardson, J.D. *et al.* (1998).

10. See Davis, L. A. (1996).

11. See US Department of Labor (1996).

12. See US Department of Commerce (1997).

13. For a fuller discussion of the economic effects of foreign direct investment, see Graham, E.M. and Krugman P.(1995). See also Florida, R. (1995).

14. See UNCTAD (1996). See also Blomstrom, M. and Kokko, A. (1997).

15. See Aitken, B. Hanson, G.D. and Harrison, A. (1994). See also Coe, D., Helpman, E. and Hoffmaister, A. (1995).

16. A 1995 survey of 189 foreign-owned enterprises established in New Zealand by KPMG, the business consultancy firm, found that 90 per cent of value-added by foreign-owned companies remains in the country - i.e., only ten percent of the profits earned by foreign firms in New Zealand were remitted offshore. The survey also showed that foreign-owned firms paid wages some 28 per cent higher than domestic companies. It is estimated that about one third of the New Zealand workforce (593,000 individuals) is employed by enterprises that are based either directly or indirectly on foreign investment.

17. See OECD (1995b).

18. See Borensztein, E., de Gregorio, J. and Lee, J. (1995).

19. See UNCTAD (1996).

20. See Commission of the European Communities (1994).

21. See Fontagné, L. (1997).

22. See WTO (1997*a*) for a survey of empirical work on this subject.

23. Chapters IV and V provide further illustrations of the economy-wide importance of services and their contribution to economic adjustment.

24. See Krueger, A. O. (1978); OECD (1985); Bhagwati, J. (1988) and Papageorgiou, D., Michaely, M. and Choski, A. (1990). See also Edwards, S. (1993), *op.cit.*

25. See OECD (1998).

26 See Jenkins, G.P. (1980).

27. See GATT (1993*a*).

28. See Commonwealth of Australia (1997), *op.cit.*

CLOUDS OVER THE MARKET OPENNESS DEBATE

Governments from across the political spectrum have pursued market liberalisation precisely because they have come to realise that the maintenance of open markets and a liberal, rules-based, trading order is in their citizens' best interest. This realisation has stemmed from a number of factors. To begin with, governments have witnessed (sometimes first hand) the costs, political and economic, of past episodes of protectionism. More importantly, they have seen the tangible benefits that the freeing-up of trade and investment regimes has delivered during the multilateral trading system's lifespan.

Yet that does not mean that recurring concerns about the alleged negative effects of liberalisation do not linger. It may be useful, therefore, to highlight five of these concerns and to outline the essential response, precisely in order to help deal with them.

■ **"Cheap labour threatens employment"**: the concern that trade with developing countries will have a major adverse impact on living standards in developed countries rests on a proposition that can carry enormous intuitive appeal: namely, that high-wage countries simply cannot compete with low-wage countries. If workers are paid $10 an hour in Country X and $1 an hour in Country Y, no one will produce anything in Country X. The so-called "pauper labour" argument is fundamentally flawed because it assumes that international competitiveness depends only on relative wages. In actual fact, firms pay attention not so much to the wage rates they pay their workers, but to labour costs per unit of output, or wages adjusted for productivity. If workers in Country X are more productive because it has superior know-how, better infrastructure, sounder management, or a larger stock of capital – human, financial and physical – such superior productivity can more than offset the effects of higher wages.

■ **"Exports are good and imports are bad"**: the mercantilist notion according to which exports are somehow preferable to imports suggests that trade is a zero-sum game. In fact it is about *mutually* beneficial exchange, which would not otherwise take place. In fact, some of the most significant welfare-enhancing gains from trade come from imports. What a country gains from trade is an ability to obtain products it wants, needs or is relatively inefficient at producing. Indeed, just as each individual works in order to buy goods and services that increases his or her family's quality of life, countries trade in order to buy goods and services abroad that are either cheaper or of better quality than those available from domestic sources.

■ **"Trade deficits are inherently worrisome"**: trade imbalances can become a rallying cry for opponents of liberalisation, who view them both as a sign of declining economic health and as a symptom of unfair trade practices in foreign markets. From an economic point of

Box 4.1

Issues in Agricultural Trade

With the **Uruguay Round Agreement on Agriculture** (URAA) agricultural products were for the first time firmly placed under multilateral trade disciplines. Non-tariff barriers were replaced by bound tariffs and disciplines were introduced on market access (tariff reductions and quotas), domestic support and export subsidies. Combined with other agreements of the Uruguay Round, particularly dispute settlement, sanitary and phythosanitary (SPS) measures and technical barriers to trade (TBT), the result was a more transparent and predictable trading environment for agricultural products.

The "systemic" change in the multilateral rules governing agricultural trade has been significant. But the effects in practical terms have not been so significant. The level of protection for agricultural products is still very high. The tariffication process often resulted in very high tariffs and the commitment levels for domestic support and export subsidies, although important in principle, are not generally very constraining. Recent studies by the OECD on the URAA have come to the conclusion that only a modest increase in agricultural trade could be expected to result over the implementation period (1995-2000)[1] and most of the increase will be within tariff rate quotas (TRQs).

A new multilateral negotiation on agriculture is due to start before 2000. The main challenge is to strengthen the existing three pillars of the URAA – market access, export subsidies and domestic support, so that "systemic" changes begin to be effective in reducing the high levels of support and protection that persist for some countries and commodities. Tariff levels need to be brought down – and in particular the very high tariff peaks need to be lowered. Export subsidies should be reduced or phased out and the exemptions from reduction commitments of certain types of domestic support need to be revisited. Administrative difficulties encountered with the implementation of TRQs need to be sorted out, the role of state trading enterprises and the use of TRQs as a market access tool need to be examined.

Nonetheless, multilateral commitments will, over time, have an important influence on the way that agricultural policy is made. Countries contemplating reform do so with one eye on the "blue" and "green" boxes that define the conditions under which domestic policy measures can be exempted from discipline, and against the prospect that the next phase of multilateral negotiations on agricultural trade will likely increase access and further limit export subsidies. While there are many factors motivating domestic policy reform, the process is inextricably linked to and reinforced by, multilateral commitments. Reforms undertaken or proposed by major OECD players in agricultural trade since the conclusion of the Uruguay Round reflect this fact.

New and challenging issues are emerging on the agricultural trade agenda, among them food safety and environmental concerns. These emerging issues have been highlighted recently by trade disputes involving divergent national regulations among OECD Member countries.

view, trade balances are primarily determined by macroeconomic factors – namely the balance between savings and investment. Countries that invest more than they save must attract foreign capital to finance their dis-saving, and the foreign capital is then used to pay for imported goods and services. This translates into a trade or current account deficit. To say that the level of trade barriers abroad has generally little to do with a country's trade balance is not to suggest that such barriers and the efforts required to dismantle them are somehow unimportant. Persistently high deficits can be a cause for concern and erode public support for maintaining open markets if they lead to a depreciation of a country's currency and apply downward pressure on living standards. That said, trade balances are a deeply flawed indicator of a country's economic health, as can be inferred by comparing the recent economic performances of Japan, which runs large trade surpluses, and the United States, which has long experienced large external deficits. The absolute size of a deficit means next to nothing in itself, its size relative to the overall importance of the national economy and its sustainability over time being what matters. The composition of trade is of arguably greater importance to a country's prosperity. Even though OECD countries may be importing more low-wage goods than before, deficits often mask the significant strengthening in their ability to compete in high-wage, high-productivity industries. Globalisation, and the concomitant increase in the volume of intra-firm trade it generates, has further blurred the economic significance of trade balances. For instance, intra-firm trade accounts for an estimated 40 per cent of the US trade deficit, yet a significant share of this relates to trade in information technology products, by far the most competitive sector in the US economy.

■ **"Only manufacturing matters"**: manufacturing employment as a share of total employment has declined continuously in industrialised countries in recent decades. This decline, which is often referred to as de-industrialisation, has paralleled the increasing global integration of markets and economies, fuelling perceptions that openness to trade and investment destroys manufacturing jobs. The steady decline in the share of employment in manufacturing in the industrial countries since the 1960s recalls the dramatic drop in agricultural employment throughout much of this century, a drop made possible by the very rapid growth of productivity in farming. Fuelled by the impact of information technologies and by new ways of organising production, similar productivity gains are at work today in manufacturing. The result is that manufacturing employment, which currently stands at 28.3 per cent of total civilian employment in OECD economies, could fall to less than 15 per cent a decade

from now, with services absorbing more than eight out of ten industrial country workers. The view that "only manufacturing matters" belies the reality of today's modern economies, in which many more people design and supply software services than produce computers. Implicit in such reasoning is the notion that manufacturing is more worthy or wealth-creating than are services. Overlooked is the fact that many service sector jobs, particularly those found in sectors that have grown fastest – finance, communication, health, professional services – pay more than many manufacturing jobs. Meanwhile, manufacturing has hardly ceased to matter: output and exports of manufactured products have grown steadily, even as their share in output and employment has been declining relative to services – reflecting consistently higher growth of measured productivity in manufacturing than in services.[2]

■ **"There is not enough time to anticipate adjustments to a more competitive environment"**: trade and investment liberalisation can be feared to involve sweeping short-term changes, leaving countries, firms and workers little or no time to anticipate and adjust to greater competitive pressures. Yet much of the story of post-war market liberalisation actually is one of incremental, progressive and negotiated change – of orderly adjustment – rather than of immediacy. Many would in fact argue that the pace of liberalisation, for example, in agriculture or textiles and apparel; where the economy-wide costs of protectionism far outweigh any benefits derived from trade restrictions, has been far too slow – illustrating once more the fact that protectionism is difficult to dismantle once it is granted (see Box 4.1).

That said, there is no denying that adjusting to a more competitive environment entails some costs, and that such distributional pains are often more up-front and "lumpy" (i.e. prone to affect specific firms, categories of workers, sectors, regions or countries), as opposed to benefits which may take longer to materialise for societies as a whole or be more diffuse in character (i.e. less tangibly visible, as when the purchasing power of wages increase due to greater access to lower-cost imports). Much of the disquiet of policy-makers and broad segments of the population about liberalisation owes to the fact that adjustment to a liberalised environment is – and in all likelihood needs to be – borne before the wider and larger tangible benefits can begin to be felt. This underscores the importance for governments to implement a set of policies whose central aim must be to shorten the time it takes for societies to adjust to changed economic circumstances[3].

NOTES

1. See OECD (1995c).

2. An important implication of continued de-industrialisation is that the overall growth of productivity and, thus, of wages and living standards, will be increasingly determined by what happens in the service sector. Reforming what are often antiquated or competition-impairing regulatory regimes; increasing investment in education and training to take full advantage of emerging technologies; and securing greater trade and investment liberalisation in all available fora, hold the key to raising productivity levels in services.

3. This cannot be done however without enhancing the ways in which governments communicate the overall benefits of market openness. In turn, this involves providing credible and persuasive answers to those that legitimately question such benefits on distributional, environmental or sovereignty grounds. The paper explores a range of possible answers to such concerns in the following three chapters.

5

MARKET OPENNESS, EARNINGS AND EMPLOYMENT

The period since the 1970s has witnessed an increasing differential between the labour market outcomes – employment and earnings – of skilled and unskilled workers in advanced economies. Some people have seen a link between this phenomenon and competition from low-wage, low-labour-standard developing countries. Trade from such sources has been portrayed as the cause of the steady disappearance of manufacturing jobs, the sharp decline in the demand for unskilled labour, and the related increase in income inequality observed in some OECD labour markets.

Concerns over adverse labour market developments ...

Other sources of anxiety arise in a globalising environment. The prospect of increased immigration and, especially, the increased mobility of capital arising from globalisation, means that trade is no longer the sole source of concern. Workers and politicians in the industrial world do not worry only about jobs lost at the hands of cheap exports from low-cost producers. They worry just as much about the possibility of companies relocating abroad in search of low wages and lax workplace standards.

... arise in a globalising environment

There is no doubt that much of the wavering support for trade and investment liberalisation observed recently in OECD public opinion reflects such underlying anxieties. Moreover, there is a risk that such anxieties can be translated into emotive appeals – from nostalgic yearnings for the way things used to be to the more troublesome reassertion of nationalist or protectionist sentiments.

That risk alone underlines the fundamental importance not only of getting the analysis right and the facts straight, but also of getting the arguments across to those who express such concerns in the first place. That means answering the basic questions at stake in the public domain.

Getting the facts straight is the key

Are concerns over a globalisation-induced social race to the bottom justified? Can trade and investment restrictions durably help those categories of workers on whom much of the burden of adjustment to a more competitive world tends to fall? And what would the likely economy-wide consequences of such restrictions be?

I. WHAT ROLE FOR TRADE?

A considerable number of empirical enquiries have explored the relationship between market openness, jobs and wages in recent years.[1] Virtually all studies agree that increased imports from developing countries *do* place downward pressure on the wages of unskilled workers relative to skilled workers, but most characterise such impacts as *modest*.

Indeed, the consensus view is that adverse labour market developments affecting low-skilled workers in OECD countries are primarily related to technology and changes in the organisational structure of firms rather than to import competition from developing countries. Economists often refer to this phenomenon as "skill-biased technological change".[2] This describes technology-driven shifts in labour demand away from less-skilled workers and toward more skilled workers. Such shifts have resulted in increased income inequality in some countries, particularly those with more flexible labour markets, and higher unemployment among unskilled workers in other countries, especially those characterised by greater labour market rigidities.[3]

Technology exerts a predominant influence on jobs and wages

Of course, trade, investment and technological progress are closely interrelated processes, and the task of determining their respective impacts is very complex. Though relatively little empirical work has to date been devoted to the issue, it is plausible that greater international competitive pressures, which in OECD countries still come mainly from trade and investment links with other industrialised countries, are accelerating the diffusion of labour-saving technologies. This almost invariably occurs to the detriment of unskilled workers – today as in the past. Evidence of similar patterns has also been found in a number of developing countries.

Imports from developing countries exert modest effects on OECD labour markets

Studies using various economic models suggest that increased trade with developing countries accounts for only about 10 to 20 per cent of the changes observed in wages and income distribution in the advanced economies.[4] Stating this fact counterfactually brings home the point more forcefully: fully 80 to 90 per cent of the changes in wages and income distribution observed of late in OECD countries are attributable to factors other than trade with developing countries.

As with the rising concerns over environmental degradation that are discussed in the following section, trade and investment liberalisation are held responsible for far more than the facts warrant on the labour front. This in turn creates the risk that the wrong policy instrument will be selected to address legitimate social and economic policy concerns – in this instance high and persistent unemployment and rising income inequality. Trade protection does nothing to upgrade the skills of people whose jobs may have been lost because of their employers' inability to compete with lower priced imports. It fails to address the root cause of this group's labour market problems. It is, however, a guaranteed way of inflicting real pain on skilled workers and of reducing the purchasing power of *all* consumers.

II. WHY TRADE IS NOT THE MAIN CAUSE

One reason the competitive threat of trade with developing countries is typically overstated is the tendency to overlook the economic importance of services. Developed economies today derive the bulk of their income – some 70 per cent of both output and employment – from service-related activities (see Figures 5.1 and 5.2). Two concrete implications flow from this observation. First, because many services are non-tradable and require close proximity between sellers and consumers, a large share of OECD workers are in the main shielded from the effects of international competition. Second, OECD countries and workers remain by far the most competitive suppliers of services worldwide. Accordingly, much of the competitive pressures associated with greater trade and

Most people work in the services sector

investment in services comes not from developing countries but from firms from other high-wage OECD countries. Studies show that the ongoing electronic commerce revolution will exert greater competitive pressures in the future, particularly for some categories of labour-intensive services such as data processing, remote inventory management and related back-office work.[5] The gains from trade are, after all, as compelling for services as for goods. Still, it bears recalling that greater competition in services typically takes the form of employment-generating *inflows* of foreign direct investment. Fully 60 per cent of world FDI flows are today directed to service activities.

Attention must therefore shift to manufacturing in order to gauge the significance of

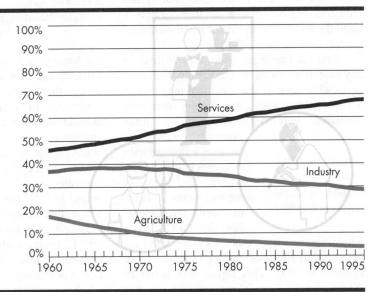

Figure 5.1

Employment by sector as a share of total civilian employment in G7 countries, 1960-96

Source: OECD (1997).

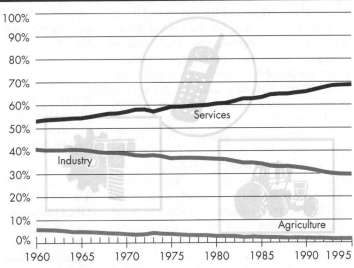

Figure 5.2

Output by sector as a share of GDP in G7 countries, 1960-95

Source: OECD (1997a).

the potential threat posed by trade with developing countries. Here again, the data do not confirm alarmist views. Figure 5.1 shows that the period since 1960 has seen a secular decline — on the order of 10 percentage points (a 25 per cent drop) in the share of manufacturing in G7 countries employment. However, rather than offering a generalised proof of the job-destruction dangers posed by trade and outward investment-induced de-industrialisation, such a decline reflects a natural evolution in the structure of advanced economies.[6]

Structural changes aside, it is difficult in any case to reconcile de-industrialisation concerns with some of the statistical magnitudes which trade with developing countries involves. Industrialised countries trade primarily with one another – that is, with countries having similar wages and endowments – when it comes to manufactured goods. For the OECD as a whole, imports from other Member countries amounted to 80 per cent of total manufactured imports in 1995. This figure was closer to 90 per cent for Canada and some 85 per cent for Member countries of the European Union, as against 70 per cent for the United States. While imports of manufactured products from emerging economies have grown steadily during the past three decades (see Figure 5.3a), they still represented a mere 1.6 per cent of OECD countries' combined output in 1995 (see Figure 5.3b).

Industrialised countries trade primarily with each other

The magnitudes depicted above do, of course, vary significantly by industry and country. A sectoral breakdown of imports from emerging economies suggests that, in most OECD countries, their incidence is relatively high in six sectors: textiles and apparel; wood products; rubber and plastics; computer equipment; transport equipment (other than aircraft and motor vehicles) and a variety of light consumer products, such as toys. All are

sectors in which OECD economies tend to be net importers, i.e. the value of imports from emerging economies exceeds the value of the sector's exports to these countries. That said, it is important to bear in mind that OECD exports of high value-added and high-skill manufactures to emerging economies, such as chemicals, pharmaceuticals, machinery and equipment, aircraft, motor vehicles and iron and steel, have grown *even faster* than their imports from emerging countries. In actual fact, total trade in manufactures between OECD countries and emerging economies is broadly balanced, a situation that has changed little since the late 1960s. Member countries actually ran a surplus equivalent to 0.25 per cent of their combined output in 1995 (see Figure 5.3c). The overall picture that emerges is thus one of growing but balanced integration of emerging countries in OECD trade, with each side supplying in textbook fashion, those goods and services it is best at producing.

Trade in manufactures between OECD and emerging economies is broadly balanced

Based on the above analysis, there is no empirical basis to conclude that trade with developing countries is chiefly responsible for the rise in unemployment and income inequality in OECD countries. That such trade is relatively balanced and represents only a small share of OECD GDP does not, of course, rule out the possibility that it may have certain adverse labour market impacts. There clearly have been industries in some OECD economies (such as, e.g., the textile and apparel sector) in which employment has been adversely affected by trade, and others in which downward pressures on wages have been felt. Pressures on the unskilled labour

Trade may have adverse labour market impacts in some sectors and regions ...

Figure 5.3

Trends in OECD manufacturing trade with emerging economies (EEs)*

a) Share of EEs in total manufacturing imports

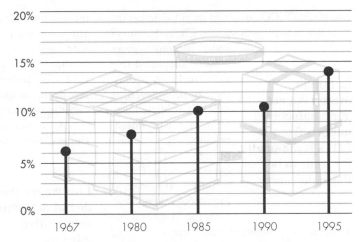

b) Imports from EEs (per cent of GDP)

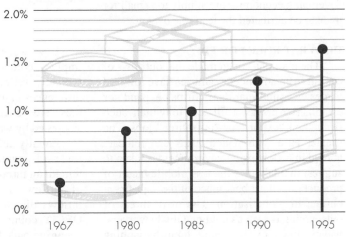

c) Net exports to EEs (per cent of GDP)

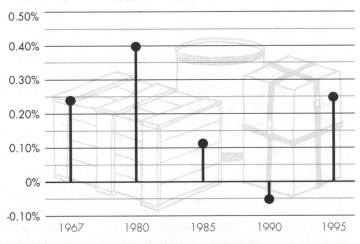

* Emerging economies comprise the following countries: Argentina; Brazil; Chile; China; Chinese Taipei; Hong Kong, China; India; Indonesia; Korea; Malaysia; Singapore; and Thailand.

Source: OECD (1997*b*).

market of OECD countries might even persist as major new players such as China, Russia or India become more closely integrated into the world economy, though such integration will just as likely mean more high-wage/ high-productivity manufacturing and service exports from OECD countries. However, as Figure 5.4 makes clear, both the level and the change in manufactured imports from developing economies are simply too small for trade to be attributed the lead role overall.

… but the overall impact of manufactured imports from LDCs is too small for trade to be the main cause

III. WHAT ROLE FOR FDI?

The claim has been made that outflows of capital from advanced countries have lowered wages as multinational firms expand or establish overseas affiliates, to which such firms then "export" or "outsource" jobs. The greater ease with which firms can relocate abroad in a globalising environment is taken to suggest that labour – the less mobile factor of production – must bear much of the adjustment burden to globalisation. The mere threat of outsourcing is seen as holding OECD workers' wages down by lessening their bargaining power.

The accelerating pace of foreign direct investment (FDI) outflows directed towards developing countries has led to a latter day revival of what used to be called the pauper labour argument: it has re-emerged as a concern that emerging countries enjoy an "unfair" competitive advantage because they are able to combine first-world skill and productivity levels with third-world wages. According to this view, firms producing in developing countries will have lower costs no matter what they choose to produce. Developing countries will thus have an advantage in producing everything unless something is done to reverse — or mitigate - the effects of wage

repression in these economies. Alongside the alleged negative employment effects of trade with low-wage countries, FDI-induced shifts in production (or the threat thereof) have been held to further undermine employment prospects in industrialised countries or the bargaining powers of workers.

As a matter of fact, careful empirical studies show that increased capital mobility, including the "outsourcing" of production to low-wage countries, as well as immigration from developing countries to the advanced economies, exert only modest effects on OECD labour markets.[7]

Low wages alone do not determine competitive advantage

Low wages do not in fact necessarily imply a competitive advantage. Low wages typically reflect low productivity. It is the differences in unit labour costs that matter, and these are generally much smaller than those suggested by wage differentials.

Equally telling is the fact that, as with trade in manufactures, FDI flows largely remain an intra-OECD affair, with 88 per cent of outflows originating in and 68 per cent of inflows directed at high-income, high-wage OECD countries (see Figure 5.5). When venturing outside the OECD area, OECD firms tend to invest in the largest or richest markets in the developing world, not in those with the lowest wages. At the top of their list are countries like Brazil and Singapore, neither of which might be considered as an ideal location for low-wage export platforms.[8] Moreover, a fair amount of FDI-driven "outsourcing" actually underpins arms-length exchanges between firms that have established global or regionally-integrated production networks, so-called intra-firm trade. The bulk of such FDI-led trade, which today accounts

As with trade, FDI remains predominantly an intra-OECD affair

for 55 per cent of world merchandise exports, once more takes place within firms located in OECD countries.[9]

Data on the activities of US multinational enterprises (MNEs), the world's most internationally active, shed additional light on the significance of outsourcing activities and the potential impact on OECD workers. Output in the foreign affiliates of US MNEs accounted for 22.9 per cent of such firms' total output in 1994, a negligible rise over the 21.9 per cent share observed in 1982. Moreover, overall employment in the foreign affiliates of US MNEs is actually a lower share of total employment in these firms today than it was in 1977.[10] Were the fears of critics of FDI being realised, such figures would be expected to have increased more significantly.

Were wages the sole determinant of MNEs' locational decisions, developing countries would presumably be attracting a significant share of FDI flows and indeed be on their way to becoming manufacturing powerhouses. The data on manufactured trade between OECD and emerging economies cited earlier belie this prediction. The fact that developing countries attract less than a third of global FDI flows suggests that factors other than wages weigh more heavily on firms' location decisions.[11] These include: proximity to the markets of key suppliers and higher-income final consumers; access to high-quality transport and telecommunications infrastructures; ready access to a highly-skilled workforce; a transparent and investor-friendly legal environment; and overall environmental quality. The greater overall endowments of developed economies – those on which their prosperity rests in the first place – also explain the observed tendency for labour productivity within multinational enterprises to be noticeably higher – up to two and half times in the case of US firms – in developed than in developing country affiliates.[12]

Factors other than wages weigh more heavily on the location decisions of firms

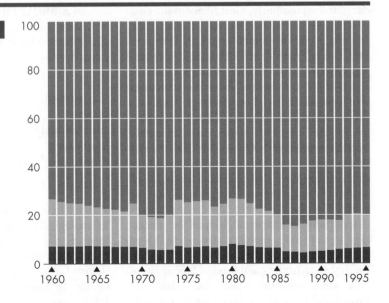

Figure 5.4

OECD manufactured imports from low, middle and high-income countries, 1960-95

(per cent of total OECD imports, current prices)

■ High-income countries

■ Middle-income countries

■ Low-income countries

Source: OECD Foreign Trade database.

Trends in foreign direct investment by major region, 1991-96 average

Source: OECD (1997*c*).

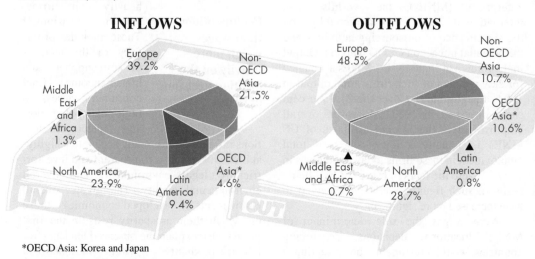

*OECD Asia: Korea and Japan

This is far from being a picture of rapid shift in production capacity towards "low wage" countries. This, of course, does not exclude the possibility, most likely in the case of countries within a regional trading area, that so-called "delocalisation" from OECD to non-OECD countries occurs with a view to reducing labour costs. Indeed, examples can be found of plants located in developing countries that operate at or above average levels of productivity found in industrialised countries, as in the case of some auto assembly operations in Mexico. Quite apart from the fact that workers in such plants tend to earn wages that are far above the national average, such examples remain the rare exception and not the rule. The fact is that the main forces determining international competitive advantage are not readily mobile on the whole. There is not, for instance, free mobility of labour. Simply stated, home and foreign labour are at best weak substitutes and, like trade and investment themselves, increasingly complement each other.

IV. VIEWING TRADE AND INVESTMENT-INDUCED DISLOCATIONS IN A BROADER CONTEXT

Even when trade and investment liberalisation leads to a bigger overall pie by expanding aggregate income and employment, they can also lead to job displacement and employment losses. However, these losses must be viewed in the context of the dislocation that occurs continually in modern economies. Just as it spawns new and improved types of work, technological change is constantly "destroying" jobs, as are domestic competition, business cycle downturns and changes in the pattern of demand. A good example of the latter is the decline in employment in defence industries felt in some countries following the end of the Cold War.

Adjustment occurs continuously in modern economies

Empirical research focusing on the US labour market has found trade responsible for less than 6 per cent of the drop in US manufacturing employment between 1978 and 1990, an amount equivalent to one per cent of total US employment.[13] In the case of Canada, the empirical evidence suggests that tariff cuts under the 1988 Canada-US Free Trade Agreement explain only 9 to 14 per cent of lost manufacturing jobs during 1989-93, the bulk of which could be traced to the combined effects of corporate restructuring that predated the FTA, a severe recession and the country's monetary policy stance during the period.[14]

Trade helps redeploy a society's productive resources

Trade creates as well as destroys jobs, easing the reabsorption of displaced workers (albeit that this may well be in different sectors). For instance, less than a third of the 155,000 workers whose jobs the US Department of Labor certified as lost because of the North American Free Trade Agreement (NAFTA) actually drew benefits under the agreement's adjustment assistance programme. This suggests that up to two-thirds of NAFTA-certified job losses were quickly reabsorbed by a buoyant domestic labour market. It should be recalled that the US economy generated some fourteen million new jobs since the NAFTA's entry into force. Equally telling is the fact that the US economy sees an estimated two million jobs turn over *every* month.[15] Similarly, Canada has reaped the rewards of early adjustment efforts as Canadian industry, spurred by improved access to the markets of its North American neighbours, has shifted resources towards more highly-skilled and technology-intensive manufactured exports.

A recent study assessing the boost to growth arising from the European Single Market Program (SMP), the most far-reaching market liberalisation initiative performed to date at the regional level, suggests that the European Union's level of output in 1994 was between 1.1 to 1.4 per cent above the level that would have prevailed without the SMP. The growth "premium" associated with EU-wide market liberalisation means that the Union's employment level in 1994 was between 300,000 and 900,000 units (equivalent to between 0.2 to 0.5 per cent of total EU employment) above the level that would have prevailed without the SMP, depending on the choice of economic model.[16] These results suggest that, without the SMP, the European Union's current labour market difficulties would have actually worsened significantly.

It needs also to be kept in mind that the chief influence of trade is not so much its direct effect on the aggregate level of employment, which over the long-term is affected also (and more fundamentally) by several other factors, but on the qualitative nature of the jobs that modern economies sustain and create. The main employment effects of trade thus come essentially from the increases they allow in competition and efficiency, and because trade and foreign direct investment both act as a spur to the overall productivity of factors of production. These *indirect* effects translate into higher growth, which in turn induces employment gains.

Trade-induced adjustment can be a powerful spur to innovation, even for traditional sectors that are heavily exposed to foreign competitive pressures and sometimes referred to as "sunset" industries.

Trade and investment liberalisation allow faster growth, which in turn sustains and creates better jobs

The somewhat fatalistic notion of sunset industries has itself become highly relative in a globalising environment, as even small- and medium-sized enterprises from regions and sectors formerly associated with industrial decline have shown an ability to become strongly integrated into world markets (see Box 5.1).

V. WHY DISTRIBUTION MATTERS

While trade and investment liberalisation can be counted on to raise world welfare in aggregate, the gains will be distributed unevenly across countries and between different sectors and groups within countries. Moreover, workers do not move easily or quickly from shrinking sectors that are competing with imports to expanding ones that are exporting, so that even when trade is balanced, there will likely be transitory problems in the labour market.

The message that open markets lead to increased welfare in the aggregate is of little consolation to people whose lives may be adversely affected by change and who may need to uproot their families in search of alternative employment. Nor does it sit well with the literature on displaced workers that emphasises that post-displacement earnings do not easily recover to pre-displacement levels, especially when workers are forced to change industries.[17]

There exist rising public concerns in a number of industrialised countries over high and persistent unemployment, widening earnings and income disparities and the accelerating pace of change brought about by globalisation. It is all the more important, therefore, that there be effective policies in place to respond to concerns that the benefits of liberalisation should not be distributed too unevenly. Policymakers must therefore take account of distributional issues and transitional costs in designing policies aimed at easing adjustments to changing economic circumstances. The challenge of ensuring a more equitable distribution of the gains from trade and investment does not stop at national borders, equity considerations being just as important internationally if the gains from more open markets are to accrue nationally (see Box 5.2).

Ensuring a more equitable distribution of the gains from market openness is a key policy challenge

From a policy perspective the crucial point is that trade, investment and technology *all* interact in ways that increase the wage premium for high-skilled workers and depress the demand for the low-skilled. The challenge for policymakers then becomes how to cope with this trend. Postponing adjustment through trade protection or restrictions on capital outflows has been amply shown by theory, history and empirical evidence to be a blind alley. Protectionism would insulate economies from the market signals that point to the need for early adjustment; inflicts damage on exporting firms by making them less competitive; hurts consumers by raising the prices of imports; and provides what are in most instances short-term and high-cost palliative relief to firms, workers and communities for whom delayed adjustment almost invariably translates into greater longer-term hardship.

Mindful of the costs of protectionism, some countries have preferred to introduce special adjustment assistance schemes which aim to compensate the losers from trade liberalisation and also to bolster political support for liberalisation initiatives. Under such schemes, displaced workers are either provided with a range of services (e.g., job retraining) designed to help them find new employment or they are compensated financially through special income maintenance payments. However, the trend in most OECD countries has been to move away from special trade adjustment assistance targeted on displaced workers [18] and to rely instead on active labour market policies open to all job seekers with employment handicaps or at risk of becoming long-term unemployed. Furthermore, the effectiveness of these measures in achieving a speedy reintegration of displaced workers back into jobs has been shown to require careful attention to programme design (see Box 5.3).[19]

Active labour market policies are needed alongside structural, macro-economic and social policies

Box 5.1

Small Can Be Beautiful:
Local and regional responses to competitive pressures in manufacturing industries

After the Second World War, an unexpected "economic miracle" took place in a number of small towns and rural areas in OECD countries when their relatively underdeveloped economies were transformed into prosperous industrial poles in a surprisingly short space of time. Examples exist in many Member countries but the "industrial districts" in Northern Italy are probably among the best known. In these areas, in the 1950s and the 1960s traditional artisans confronted with a rapid increase in cross-border trade managed to transform their low-productivity and labour-intensive workshops into small, competitive industrial firms. Skilled workers laid off from factories previously involved in war production started up factories by themselves, assisted by the expansion of domestic and international demand. By the 1970s, foremen and maintenance workers with production management experience were encouraged to become subcontractors by large firms facing decline because of international competition and in search of flexibility and lower costs. As a result of these processes, hundreds of small firms belonging to the same vertically integrated sectors, but specialised in different phases of the production chain, became concentrated in small regions. These locations are currently among the richest and most dynamic in the country — indeed in Europe — in terms of both per capita income and employment growth.

Local industrial districts account for close to 30 per cent of total Italian employment (43 per cent of employment in manufacturing) and, in 1994, contributed a remarkable 43 per cent of Italian exports. Between 1981 and 1994, employment growth in the districts increased by 20 per cent, some three and a half times greater than for Italy as a whole. A particularly remarkable trend concerns producer services

employment, such as accounting, software applications, personnel recruitment, transport and distribution logistics, which grew by close to 65 per cent over the period. Studies show that, even in periods of recession, job creation, real wages and returns on investment have all been consistently higher in these local industrial districts than elsewhere. This is striking given that many of these areas specialise in manufactured goods such as textiles, clothing and footwear that are often considered to be vulnerable to cheap imports. Yet, the area of Castellgoffredo, for example, with 180 small firms, continues to produce 61 per cent of total European production of stockings. Sassuolo is the leading area in Europe for the production of ceramic tiles. Prato, a well-known textile district with 5,990 firms and 38,080 employees, produces 64 per cent of national exports of wool fabrics. And Carpi, with 2,068 knitting and clothing firms, having an average of 5 employees each, has total sales of US$1.3 billion. These examples illustrate how it is possible to maintain robust economic and employment performance in so-called "sunset" industries even in a more open competitive environment.

While the success of industrial districts is a useful reminder that the very notion of sunset industries is debatable, such success is not limited to traditional goods. High growth "sunrise" industries also tend to concentrate in specific locations. Notable high-tech clusters include Boston's Route 128 (minicomputers), the San Francisco Bay Area (biotechnology), Montreal, Canada (computer software), Cambridge, UK (scientific instruments) and Hamamatsu, Japan (musical instruments). As in Italian districts, these areas mix strong output and employment growth with good working conditions and an emphasis on training.

Effective active labour market policies can play an important role in accommodating the potential dislocating effects of trade and investment liberalisation, but they cannot play this role alone and in isolation from other structural, macro-economic and social policies. In particular, in an environment of rigid labour and product markets, active labour market policies will typically only be able to play a relatively modest role. A much broader strategy is called for in order to shorten the "adjustment cycle" of OECD economies, raise workforce mobility and upgrade the skills of workers.

These objectives were addressed by the OECD Jobs Study which stressed the need for "a balanced mix of policies which mutually reinforce innovative and adaptive capacity".[20] The ten principal policy orientations of the OECD Jobs Strategy, agreed by all Member countries, therefore, provide the proper basis for coping with structural changes, including those stemming from trade and investment liberalisation (see Box 5.4). Evidence shows that, by implementing the Jobs Strategy in full, a number of OECD countries have been able to durably reduce structural unemployment rates.[21] Greater product market flexibility also helps economies cope with the pressures of globalisation and remain competitive. The OECD Report on Regulatory Reform outlined steps governments can take to reduce regulatory burdens and improve the quality and cost effectiveness of regulations that remain.[22]

Social protection policies may also need to be reoriented towards better meeting the needs of groups who are not benefiting from the rise in prosperity associated with increased trade and technological developments. Social protection systems can ensure that those who lose their jobs due to liberalisation or other reasons, are insured against excessive income losses over the period during which they search for a new job. Thus, one effect of globalisation could be to *increase* the demand for social protection[23]

A modern, efficiently administered welfare state can reduce resistance to change and new working practices, enhancing productivity and the attractiveness of the country as a business location. Increased international trade and investment is, thus, an additional reason to

---

Box 5.2

Spreading the gains from market openness

There is a presumption that in most instances the overall gains accruing from market liberalisation outweigh the disruptive effects. But that only guarantees that an economy's average standard of living rises. The problem is that an economy's median standard of living, that at which most middle-class income earners can be found, may not rise. Hence, the importance of addressing the question of how to ensure that the gains from global integration are diffused as broadly as possible.

Diffusion raises the age-old challenge of reconciling the competing objectives of allocative efficiency and distributive justice. The key is for societies to strike internal bargains that reflect a politically supportable balance between the two. Bargains that allow those at risk from open markets to be compensated, for instance, through improved job training programmes, are essential to maintaining domestic support for further liberalisation. For market liberalisation to enjoy broader and continued support, it is important not only that compensation be available but that it actually take place.

Five decades of multilateral trade diplomacy suggest that similar bargains are required for spreading gains across countries. The challenge is to agree on negotiating agendas that are broad enough to attract countries at different levels of development to join the fray and allow compensatory bargains across issue areas – agriculture, textiles, services, intellectual property, investment, environment – to be struck. Without such compensatory bargains, the gains to the small number of large gainers could be too large relative to those of the large number of small gainers and the few losers. The end result would be similar to that observed domestically: namely, the risk of seeing support for further liberalisation eroded.

improve the efficiency of public social protection systems, rather than a rationale to reduce overall levels of protection. There is no inevitable connection between increased openness and less social protection, but failure to assist those who are adversely affected by competition risks – in particular, the unskilled – can lead to an increase in protectionist sentiment.

The key is for all such policies to be implemented in such a way as to promote adjustment and harness the gains from liberalisation, rather than diluting such gains by impeding the trend toward market integration. A central policy message must be that resistance to adjustment is generally less pronounced in faster growing economies, and that faster growing economies are typically characterised by greater, not lesser, degrees of market openness.

Resistance to change is less pronounced in faster growing economies

VI. CONCERNS
OVER LABOUR STANDARDS

The last few years have seen growing attention to the issue of trade, investment and labour standards. In a context of intensified international competition, instances of child labour exploitation or of denial of rights to freedom of association and collective bargaining in some developing countries has been viewed, not only as a human rights matter, but also as providing developing countries with "unfair" competitive advantages.

The issues surrounding labour standards and trade and investment liberalisation have been greatly clarified in the last several years, thanks to the emergence of a body of research and extensive international discussion. In this regard considerable progress has been made in identifying and focusing on the more precise or "core"

The debate over trade and labour standards has been greatly clarified in recent years

---

Box 5.3

Coping with change: recent directions in active labour market policies

The principal objective of active labour market policies (ALMPs) is to assist the unemployed and first-time job seekers in ways that ensure they can compete successfully for new jobs. Active policies comprise a wide range of measures including job placement services, training programmes and subsidised employment in both the public and private sectors. If successful, these policies will reduce the duration of spells of unemployment, ensure that labour is relocated speedily from declining to expanding economic activities and raise future earnings. By helping the unemployed to adjust to new market conditions, ALMPs have an equity objective while, at the same time, they aim to improve the allocative efficiency of the labour market.

Income support during unemployment is a form of assistance which has some efficiency-enhancing effect, such as financing productive job search, but this effect is not particularly strong. This is the reason why income-support programmes (e.g., unemployment and related welfare benefits) are usually referred to as "passive" labour market policies. Recent experience has shown that, during prolonged periods of income support, there is a real risk that many of the unemployed will become discouraged in looking for work; employers also tend to use long-term unemployment as a negative signal in hiring decisions. This can easily lead to a situation of "benefit dependency".

(continued on following page)

Box 5.3 (continued)

Effectiveness of active measures not always guaranteed

However, evaluation research in several OECD countries has shown that many training and retraining programmes for displaced workers, for instance, often do not achieve their stated objectives for most workers. Even more telling was the experience in some Nordic countries and the eastern part of Germany where huge training and employment programmes were introduced in the early 1990s (albeit in rather different circumstances) to mitigate severe labour market shocks. It soon became obvious that these programmes essentially played the role of a holding operation for the unemployed or served to re-establish benefit entitlements for them rather than enhancing their employability.

Directions of reform

OECD countries now attach a high priority to trying to make active measures more effective and to reorient their spending towards those measures that do work. One route towards enhancing the effectiveness of ALMPs is to integrate – possibly in "one-stop" employment offices – the three basic functions of job placement, administration of unemployment benefits and referral of job seekers to ALMPs. The common objective of all three functions should be to prevent the drift of job seekers into long-term unemployment and social exclusion.

Another direction of reform is to introduce market signals into the operations of the public employment service (PES), the key institution in most OECD countries for the delivery of active measures. In order to measure PES performance objectively, it is necessary to have an external benchmark such as a price tag which can be attached to the services provided. Since a market price will only emerge in an environment where several service providers compete with each other, many OECD countries have disbanded the monopoly role of the PES, or they have out-contracted certain PES services, such as training, to a range of public and private providers. Australia has even gone so far as to make the whole range of PES services, including case management for the long-term unemployed, contestable in a market environment.

Converging trends in adjustment assistance

In comparing policy approaches between European and non-European countries, it is striking that, historically, Europe only very rarely resorted to labour market programmes specifically targeted on displaced workers whereas such targeted programmes have been quite frequent in the United States, Canada and Australia. The typical European response to major structural adjustment shocks was not programme-oriented and did not rely on labour supply adjustments alone. Instead, the emphasis was on "concerted action" between all parties concerned, the establishment of "social plans" and the setting up of ad hoc bodies to deal with the various aspects of the adjustment shock. Often this approach resulted in job-creation initiatives and regional and sector-specific policy interventions.

In recent years, a certain convergence in policy orientation has occurred. Very few programmes still exist in the non-European countries which are only available for displaced workers. This has removed the difficulty of denying programme access to workers who do not qualify as "displaced", yet require urgent assistance because of serious employment handicaps. In Europe, sector-specific interventions and job creation measures as a response to dislocations have become less frequent. This has lowered the risks of misallocation, slowing the speed of labour market adjustment to structural change.

These trends suggest that a well-developed infrastructure of ALMPs accessible to all who need assistance and which improves the allocative efficiency of the labour market is a promising approach to cope with future change. However, recent experience has shown also that active labour market policies need constant monitoring and evaluation, otherwise there is a risk that they gradually lose their effectiveness and no longer achieve their objectives.

labour standards at issue. There is greater international consensus on these – which relate mainly to human rights (i.e. the elimination of child labour, the prohibition of forced labour, freedom of association, the right to organise and bargain collectively, and non-discrimination in employment). By concentrating on these, much has been done to assuage earlier concerns that attention to these issues was motivated by a wish to target the lower wage structure of dynamic exporting countries. Subsequent discussion has underlined that governments have no such intention, and that there is in fact no calling into question the fundamentals of trade and investment liberalisation. It is more an issue of overall policy coherence and the more practical matter of determining the most effective way to enhance implementation of core labour standards.

Such a practical orientation has undoubtedly been shaped by the attention paid to the actual empirical relationship between trade, investment, employment and labour standards.[24] Some of the most salient conclusions of recent OECD work are that:

Key findings of recent OECD research

■ theoretical analysis suggests that, in general, trade improves aggregate economic welfare, irrespective of whether or not core standards are observed by all trading partners;

■ standard trade models show that patterns of specialisation are likely to be determined by fundamental factors such as relative factor endowments, technology and economies of scale;

■ empirical research suggests that there is no correlation at the aggregate level between real-wage growth and the degree of observance of freedom-of-association rights;

■ there is no evidence that low-standards countries enjoy a better global export performance than high-standards countries;

■ a detailed analysis of US imports of textile products (for which competition from low-standards countries is thought to be most intense) suggests that imports from high-standards countries account for a large share of the US market. Moreover, on average, the price of US imports of textile products does not appear to be associated with the degree of enforcement of child labour standards in exporting countries;

■ some cases have been recorded where governments appear to deny core standards to workers or deliberately do not enforce them with the aim of improving sectoral trade competitiveness or attracting investment into export-processing zones (EPZs); the expected economic gains from such a strategy are, however, likely to prove short-lived and could be outweighed in the longer term by the economic costs associated with low core standards;

■ an analysis of selected trade liberalisation episodes does not prove unambiguously whether trade reforms or freer association rights came first. There is no evidence that freedom-of-association rights worsened in any of the countries that liberalised trade. Nor is it apparent that the promotion of these rights impeded a subsequent trade liberalisation. The strongest finding is that there is a positive association over time between successfully sustained trade reforms and improvements in core standards;

■ while core labour standards may not be systematically absent from the location decisions of OECD investors in favour of non-OECD destinations, aggregate FDI data suggest that core labour standards are not important determinants in the majority of cases. In these circumstances, host countries may be able to enforce core labour standards without risking negative repercussions on FDI flows. Observance may work as an incentive to raise productivity through investment in human and physical capital.

Box 5.4

The OECD Jobs Strategy: key recommendations

1. Set macroeconomic policy such that it will both encourage growth and, in conjunction with good structural policies, make it sustainable.

2. Enhance the creation and diffusion of technological know-how by improving frameworks for its development.

3. Increase flexibility of working-time (both short-term and lifetime) voluntarily sought by workers and employers.

4. Nurture an entrepreneurial climate by eliminating impediments to, and restrictions on, the creation and expansion of enterprises.

5. Make wage and labour costs more flexible by removing restrictions that prevent wages from reflecting local conditions and individual skill levels, in particular of younger workers.

6. Reform employment security provisions that inhibit the expansion of employment in the private sector.

7. Strengthen the emphasis on active labour market policies and reinforce their effectiveness.

8. Improve labour force skills and competence through wide-ranging changes in education and training systems.

9. Reform unemployment and related benefit systems – and their interaction with the tax system – such that societies' fundamental equity goals are achieved in ways that impinge far less on the efficient functioning of labour markets.

10. Enhance product market competition so as to reduce monopolistic tendencies and weaken insider-outsider mechanisms, while also contributing to a more innovative and dynamic economy.

The OECD study also noted that these results imply that concerns expressed by certain developing countries that core standards would negatively affect their economic performance or their international competitive position are unfounded; indeed, it is theoretically possible that the observance of core standards would strengthen the long-term economic performance of all countries.

It may be noted that recent additional empirical work has in fact shown that where labour standards have been found to have measurable consequences for flows of foreign direct investment in manufacturing, the evidence actually shows that low labour standards deter, rather than attract, FDI.[25]

Low labour standards deter, rather than attract, FDI

Overall, this has proved to be an issue where the process of international discussion and debate has, in fact, advanced the substantive concerns about the human rights aspects of core labour standards, yet avoided the parallel worry that the issue could lead to protectionist reactions. This has been underlined by the WTO Singapore Ministerial where it was agreed that:

"We renew our commitment to the observance of internationally recognized core labour standards. The International Labour Organization (ILO) is the competent body to set and deal with these standards, and we affirm our support for its work in promoting them. We believe that economic growth and development, fostered by increased trade and further trade liberalization, contribute to the promotion of these standards. We reject the use of labour standards for protectionist purposes, and agree that the comparative advantage of countries, particularly low-wage developing countries, must in no way be put into question. In this regard, we note that the WTO and ILO Secretariats will continue their existing collaboration".

Governments will need to exercise continued vigilance in ensuring that legitimate concerns over core labour standards and human

Box 5.5

Broader consensus on how to promote core labour standards

Four years of intense international discussions on labour standards-related matters have resulted in significant progress among governments on at least two key points: the identification of those labour standards that would be promoted internationally; and effective ways of carrying this out.

Which labour standards?

There is now broad consensus that this list should be restricted to four categories of "core" standards, which embody basic human rights and are "internationally recognised":

■ freedom of association and collective bargaining, i.e. the right of workers to form organisations of their own choice and to negotiate freely their working conditions with their employers;

■ elimination of exploitative forms of child labour, such as bonded labour and forms of child labour that put the health and safety of children at serious risk; and

■ prohibition of forced labour, in the form of slavery and compulsory labour;

■ non-discrimination in employment, i.e., the right to equal respect and treatment for all workers.

What action to promote these standards?

Participants at the 1995 Copenhagen World Social Summit agreed to voluntarily promote adherence to the provisions of the ILO Conventions which deal with the above standards[26]. There is indeed wide recognition that the ILO has a primary role in promoting these standards and this institution is now considering how it can enhance both its normative and implementation capacities.

A broadening consensus appears to be emerging on two important principles that should underpin discussions of how best to promote core labour standards:

■ these mechanisms must not put the comparative advantage of low-wage countries into question, in other words, have disguised protectionist objectives;

■ nor should they take the form of trade sanctions.

---

rights abuses are dealt with through appropriate policies and institutions and are not used as a means of backtracking from the path of market liberalisation. Constructive ways forward are being considered through increased international dialogue. These include reinforcing the ILO, notably by strengthening

Focusing on constructive solutions

its transparency-enhancing surveillance powers. Nor should the power of the market itself be overlooked, whether this is through such measures as adoption of labels or firm-specific voluntary codes of conduct. In today's age of mass communication, consumer reluctance to buy goods that are produced under exploitative labour conditions can create a powerful incentive to alter firm behaviour and, in turn, for the governments concerned to redress the problems.

NOTES

1. For a review of this literature, see Slaughter, M. and Swaigel, P. (1997). See also chapter 4 of OECD (1997*b*).

2. See Lawrence, R.Z. and Slaughter, M. (1993); Neven, D. and Wyplosz, C. (1996) and Ravenga, A. (1992).

3. See Cline, W. (1997) and Rodrik, D. (1997).

4. See Slaughter, M. and Swaigel, P. (1997), *op.cit.*

5. See OECD (1997*l*).

6. For a useful synthesis of the main arguments in the debate over de-industrialisation, see IMF (1997).

7. When considering the link between immigration and labour market performance, it is worth bearing in mind that seven out of eight immigrants who have settled in OECD countries arrive through highly regulated channels that are there to ensure that the immigration concerned also serves the needs of the host country. See World Bank (1995) and Papademetriou, D.G. (1998).

8. Nearly half of FDI flows directed to non-OECD countries have gone to one country — China , fuelled in large part by the rapid growth of its domestic market. Of this total, nearly two thirds is estimated to have come from Hong Kong, China and Chinese Taipei.

9. See UNCTAD (1997).

10. See chapter 5 of Lawrence, R.Z. (1996).

11. Several studies have shown wages not to be a significant determinant of FDI patterns. A number of such studies were surveyed in UNCTC (1992).

12. See Lawrence, R.Z. (1996), *op.cit.*

13. See Sachs and Shatz (1994).

14. See Gaston and Trefler, D. (1997).

15. See Lawrence, R.Z. and Litan, R.E. (1997).

16. See Commission of European Communities (1996*c*).

17. See Jacobson, L.S., Lalonde, R.J. and Sullivan, D.G. (1993).

18. The United States being the main exception.

19. See OECD (1994).

20. See OECD (1994), *op.cit.*

21. See OECD (1997n) and OECD (1997*i*).

22. See OECD (1997*k*).

23. Rodrik (1997) has claimed that there is empirical evidence for such an effect. In particular, the greater is the product of the openness of an economy (as proxied by the sum of exports and imports as a percentage of GDP) and the variation in terms of trade, the greater has been the growth in social expenditure.

24. See OECD (1996*b*). See also Rodrik, D. (1996).

25. See Rodrik, D. (1997), *op.cit.*

26. It should be noted that there are no existing ILO conventions on the exploitation of child labour, although Member countries are currently discussing how to establish one.

6

TRADE, INVESTMENT AND ENVIRONMENTAL INTEGRITY

Environmental issues have grown in prominence on both the domestic and international policy agendas, and today the protection and preservation of national, regional and global environments competes with trade and other issues for public and media attention.

Like the debate over trade with low-wage countries, the liberalisation-environment interface can be prone to divide developed and developing countries. The fear has been expressed that lower standards in the developing countries will lead to a "race to the bottom" in the environmental standards of developed nations. This reflects a concern, in turn, that competitiveness factors could inhibit the ability of developed countries to maintain high standards over the longer-term. There are also fears that firms would move from developed to developing countries in order to take advantage of the lower environmental standards (and presumably, lower operating costs) which exist there.

Fears of an environmental race to the bottom ...

In the face of such concerns – some of which go so far as to include an opposition to further liberalisation – it is essential to analyse, as objectively as possible, what the facts of the situation are. Are environmental standards in developed countries actually likely to fall in response to heightened competitive pressures from developing nations? Do developed

country firms actually relocate to the developing world in order to take advantage of lower environmental standards there? Does liberalisation impair countries' capacity to institute measures designed to maintain high levels of environmental protection? These are some of the core questions addressed in this and the following chapter.

... call for a careful examination of the facts

I. MARKET LIBERALISATION AND THE ENVIRONMENT: COMPLEMENTARITY

Among the reasons why the relationship between market openness and the environment is at issue is the basic question of whether more trade and investment is inherently bad for the environment. Some argue that increased business activity resulting from trade and investment liberalisation (or, for that matter, from economic growth itself) inevitably results in increased consumption and production and, therefore, in lowered environmental quality.

Sound environmental policies are key to maximising the benefits open markets can bring

When environmental policies are set at appropriate levels, available evidence suggests that trade and investment activities will usually have a positive impact on the environment.[1] This is because trade and investment promote both a more efficient allocation of resources (including environmental resources) at the same time that they contribute to economic growth. The result should be increased social welfare which, in turn, generally reinforces demands for improved environmental policies.

However, when environmental policies are not set at appropriate levels, usually because the prices of environmental resources do not reflect their true social cost, trade and investment activities can aggravate existing environmental problems. (See Box 6.1 for the example of subsidised coal or fisheries resources.) In such situations, the extra environmental costs associated with trade and investment liberalisation need to be weighed against the efficiency gains anticipated from the liberalisation process. Only if the latter is greater than the former is it certain that liberalisation will lead to a net welfare gain. Of course, many factors will influence the mix of benefits and costs found in particular countries, at different stages of development, and under different policy and market conditions.

There is little disagreement that trade and investment liberalisation will cause the level of economic activity to increase (so-called *scale effects*) as societies move up the income ladder. More goods and services will be produced, transported, consumed, and disposed of than would otherwise be the case. That is, after all, what motivates mutually beneficial exchanges in the first place. There is a legitimate concern that, in the absence of appropriate environmental policies, those additional economic activities can contribute to environmental degradation.

However, other factors may be at work to abate such effects or, indeed, generate positive effects that outweigh them. And, of course, appropriate environmental policies may in fact be applied. There is no reason, therefore, to believe that environmental worsening necessarily follows from increased trade or investment.

One major factor to bear in mind on this point is the empirical observation that the demand for environmental quality rises as societies move up the income ladder.[2] Evidence shows that governments will indeed face increasing popular pressure to move in the direction of greater spending on environmental integrity as incomes rise.[3] Studies that look both at the *quantity* of resources spent on environmental protection and the *quality* of the institutional machinery

Box 6.1

Subsidy reform as a win-win solution on the trade-environment front

Although subsidies have been a major issue in international trade negotiations for decades because of their trade-distorting effects, it is only in the past decade that their negative impacts on the environment have been widely recognised. Subsidies that encourage the extraction or use of natural resources rank among the most environmentally damaging subsidies, both because they tend to be larger (relative to the value of production) than subsidies in the manufacturing sector, and because their environmental effects are more far-reaching. Subsidies to producers or users of energy, food crops, fish or timber often create severe distortions of international trade as well as increasing environmental degradation. These subsidies send false price signals to both investors and consumers that encourage overuse of resources and the adoption or excessive use of environmentally damaging technologies or production techniques. They are thus objectionable both on general economic efficiency and fair competition grounds. Reducing and eliminating such subsidies is an ideal example of how trade liberalisation and environmental protection can be clearly complementary.

Some recent examples illustrate these points. Until the mid-1990s, the coal mining industry in the UK was protected from competition from other fuels and from imports through

(continued on following page)

Box 6.1 (continued)

government-brokered contracts between producers and the electricity generators. The phasing out of this support yielded several benefits for the environment. First, it reduced various local effects of mining: waste piles, ground subsidence and methane emissions. In fact, much of the domestic consumption was replaced not by coal but by natural gas, a much cleaner-burning fuel. Furthermore, the ending of the local purchase obligation allowed the electric utilities to retire old, relatively inefficient, power stations that had been kept on-line in part to provide an outlet for domestic coal. Thus, both the average efficiency and emission performance of the country's power plants improved after liberalisation.

Subsidies to fish harvesting provide another telling example. Such subsidies have a negative impact from a conservation standpoint because they encourage overcapitalisation of the sector and promote overfishing, all of which in turn exacerbate already difficult problems of fisheries management. In addition, they induce a distorted market equilibrium, by lowering costs and prices, encouraging fishing activity and stimulating demand. Norway once provided a rich menu of subsidies to its fishing sector,

including price support for fish sales, subsidies to reduce operational costs and financing for new fishing vessels. These subsidies, which peaked at close to Nkr 1.5 billion (US$240 million) in 1990, have since fallen by a remarkable 90 per cent. During this same period, Norway introduced a number of improvements to its fisheries management system. Since then, sea fish stocks in Norwegian waters have steadily improved, landings have increased and the industry has become leaner and more profitable. Removing subsidies to fishing, combined with improved management, thus provides yet another example of a "win-win" situation – for the environment as well as for economic efficiency.

Subsidy reform does not divide developing countries from industrialised ones, as is the case of many other trade and environment challenges. Most of the environmentally damaging subsidies have been provided by industrialised countries, and developing countries would benefit economically from subsidy reform both in their own countries and in the markets of OECD countries. So subsidy reform may be expected to receive greater attention in the coming years than it has in the past.

---

involved in implementing environmental policy conclude that the overall environmental performance of countries is positively associated with rising per capita income levels, the security of property rights, and general administrative efficiency (i.e. well functioning legal and regulatory systems, see Figure 6.1).

The fact is that the world's richest nations also happen to be those whose firms operate under the most stringent environmental regulations in today's global economy. Standards for air and water quality in OECD countries are much higher today than they were 50 years ago, even though the share of OECD trade and investment in these countries' GDP is higher than ever. It should also be recalled that the quality of water and sewage treatment in European cities was no better at the beginning

of the twentieth century than it is now in many developing countries. The pollution norms applying to industries in OECD countries were, until the Second World War, similarly deficient – a situation which prevailed in much of Central and Eastern Europe until the fall of the Berlin Wall less than a decade ago.

The world's richest nations maintain the toughest environmental regulations

Although the demand for environmental quality tends to rise with incomes, it should be acknowledged that the precise consequences of such a link are not clear cut. On the one hand, there is the hypothesis that increased levels generate *additional* support for environmental protection, thereby reducing the environmental intensity of current production, so that the negative scale effects could turn out to be less than anticipated. In effect, pollution may exhibit a "U- shaped" pattern with respect to economic development, rising in the early stages of growth, and eventually falling as the demand for environmental quality grows faster than the economy itself. On the other hand, several observers remain unconvinced. They consider that the inflection point on the inverted "U-curve" in some developing countries may be at very much higher income levels, so the level of income in some countries might need to increase significantly before new demands for environmental improvements begin to take effect. Accordingly, the environmental intensity of production (and hence, the risk of environmental degradation) in these countries may continue rising for some time. For another thing, not all forms of pollution decrease with economic growth. Projections of the world economy in 2020, for example, show that increasing consumption of fossil fuels and associated emissions are likely to accompany the anticipated shift in economic weight from OECD countries to the non-OECD economies.[4] Whether or not sustainable abatement technology exists is also a factor to be borne in mind. Determining the net environmental effect of market liberalisation is, therefore, a question that has not yet been fully answered by existing research.

There is more research to be done on the net environmental effects of market liberalisation

Be that as it may, in instances where rising incomes do lead to greater demands for environmental improvements, trade and investment liberalisation can make a strong contribution to helping meet environmental objectives. Trade and investment liberalisation will generate new resources to help reduce poverty, which is often the underlying cause of environmental degradation in many developing countries (along with unsustainable rates of population growth), as well as to pay for the prevention or clean-up of pollution where societies decide to "spend" some of their gains from liberalisation on environmental protection.

Liberalisation should facilitate the dissemination of "cleaner" technologies

There is also some evidence that, once a country begins to industrialise, trade and investment liberalisation helps to make the structure of its economy less pollution-intensive than in those countries whose economies remain relatively closed (so-called *structural effects*).[5] In particular, freer trade helps to promote the transition from heavy resource-processing sectors to light manufacturing ones (at least at middle-income levels). One structural shift that has occurred as a result of trade and investment liberalisation initiatives taken to date, is the increased participation of the newly-industrialised economies in the international economy, coupled with their general shift away from primary commodity production, and toward resource-processing, light manufacturing and service activities. The latter all tend to be less environmentally-intensive than the former.

Trade and investment in environmentally-preferred products (so-called *product effects*), particularly eco-efficient capital equipment and its accompanying "clean" production technologies (so-called *technology effects*), are other important mechanisms through which liberalisation can benefit the environment. For example, trade and investment liberalisation will expand the potential market for less environmentally-intensive final products (e.g., low-emission vehicles). It will also tend to improve access to environmentally-preferable raw material inputs (e.g., low-sulphur coal).[6]

In addition, the signals that environmentally-conscious consumers – citizens, public interest groups, governments – send to producers provide the latter with potentially-

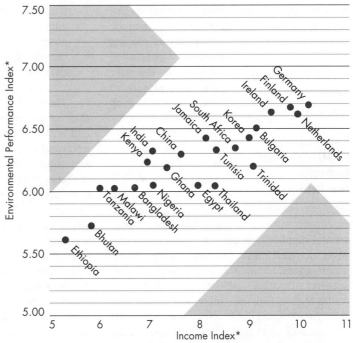

Figure 6.1

Linkages between environmental performance and income

Source:
Dasgupta, S. et al. (1995).

*Environmental performance on income indices as calculated by the World Bank (1995)

---

powerful incentives to change the nature of the products on offer or the manner by which these products are produced. An open trade and investment system transmits such signals and can accelerate change in the right direction.[7] As an example of this, the world market for environmental goods and services, the most competitive suppliers of which are located in OECD countries, is expected to experience rapid trade, investment and high-skilled employment growth in the coming decade. Nevertheless, this growth remains hampered by tariffs and a range of other barriers (see Box 6.2).

From a developing country perspective, long-standing trade restrictions and trade distortions maintained by OECD countries,

The rising influence of consumer advocacy

such as high tariffs on processed commodities, non-tariff barriers, and production and export subsidies, hold back income growth, and may have the perverse effect of encouraging developing countries to fall back on alternative production possibilities, such as intensifying the output of natural resource-based commodities, in order to raise their export earnings. Concurrently, restrictions on foreign ownership associated with inward investments, or restrictions on imports which embody modern foreign-based technologies, are often maintained by developing countries. Such restrictions act as an impediment to transfers of cost and waste reducing technologies and production methods.

When developing countries with outward-oriented trade and investment policies are compared to countries with less open policies, studies indicate that the former appear to have achieved comparatively improved environmental standards. For example, recent studies for several Latin American countries, and for some eighty developing countries, concluded that pollution intensity grew most rapidly in those countries which had remained relatively closed to world market forces.[8] This suggests that openness to foreign competition is likely to translate into increased pressure for more stringent environmental standards. In part, this comes from the need to sell into markets with higher environmental standards and "greener" consumers. It also reflects the fact that multinational firms are increasingly adopting world-wide standards for environmental performance and placing stricter environmental demands on their suppliers (see Box 6.3).

Studies show that pollution intensity has grown faster in countries that have remained relatively closed to world market forces

As the foregoing discussion suggests, there are, real challenges to be met. There is, however, no reason to be overly pessimistic about the scope for "decoupling" the relationship between economic growth and negative environmental impacts, for instance, through technological advances, structural reforms or intensified regulatory co-operation.

It is also clear that trade and investment liberalising policies are only one aspect of the overall growth process. Nevertheless, empirical evidence points to the positive contribution that on balance, trade and investment liberalisation can make to environmental protection. This contribution will operate through four main channels:

- improved efficiency of resource allocation and use;
- reduction or removal of existing trade- and investment-related distortions and restrictions which already damage the environment;
- improvements in, and the transfer, adoption and diffusion of, environmentally-friendly technologies, allowing each additional good or service produced to generate less pollution; and
- increased international availability of environmental goods and services.

Three broad policy conclusions can be drawn from the above discussion. First, strong and natural complementarities exist between trade and investment policies on the one hand, and more efficient environmental policies, on the other. Rather than foregoing the benefits of trade and investment liberalisation, therefore, efforts should be intensified to design environmental policies that value environmental resources correctly, and to implement those policies more effectively. Second, trade and investment is more likely to raise environmental standards in developing countries than lower them in the industrialised ones. And third, more liberalised trade and investment policies will make possible the new incomes and new resources needed to ensure political support for higher environmental standards than exist today.

II. AN FDI-LED RACE TO THE BOTTOM? WHAT THE FACTS SHOW

Another aspect of concern over the environmental consequences of market openness relates more to foreign direct investment than to trade, with a main focus on so-called "pollution havens". There have been fears that firms will relocate their plants in search of lower environmental standards, with FDI outflows "exporting" jobs and increased business resistance to enacting or upgrading home country environmental standards on competitiveness grounds.

There is no denying that some countries could be attracted by the idea of relaxing the level or the enforcement of their environmental laws in order to attract certain types of foreign direct investment. Similarly, some firms in specific pollution-intensive industries may be more sensitive to the costs of complying with more stringent environmental standards.

Box 6.2

Liberalising markets for environmental goods and services

The removal of barriers to trade in environmental goods and services offers a direct and obvious means of simultaneously promoting the dual goals of environmental protection and economic growth. By improving access to state-of-the-art technologies embodied in traded goods and services at lower prices, a golden opportunity presents itself to "stretch" the global environmental budget.

Private sector surveys have estimated that sales for the environment industry currently stand at some $420 billion. This is expected to grow to $600 billion by 2010. This would place the environmental goods and services industry roughly on par with the pharmaceutical or information technology industries. Further, industry experts foresee continued growth of demand for environmental goods and services at an unprecedented rate throughout the 21st century. In turn, such growth recalls the need to make further headway both in opening up government procurement markets world-wide, which remain fortresses of discrimination, and in tackling the distortive effects of bribery and corruption in international commerce.

In view of the tremendous unsatisfied demand for basic infrastructure especially (but not exclusively) in developing countries, including in waste and water management and air pollution controls, the need for the environmental goods and servicesindustry to offer value for money takes on

added importance. The expansion of international environmental standards, privatisation and deregulation of utilities such as water supply and electricity generation will all likely feed demand for environmental goods and services. For all these reasons, the industry is expected to become increasingly internationalised and trade-oriented. In turn, increased competition from open markets spurs innovation, particularly important in this sector which is technology and knowledge-intensive.

However, the sector has not been the focus of extensive liberalisation discussions. Only modest progress was achieved under the WTO General Agreement on Trade in Services, under which forty-seven countries undertook binding liberalisation commitments. In part this is because environmental goods and services have not until recently been recognised as a well-defined or separate sector. Recent analytical work in the OECD has contributed to defining its contours — covering both "end-of-pipe" and process-based technologies and goods. More recently, leaders of the Asia-Pacific Economic Co-operation forum (APEC) committed to supporting liberalisation negotiations in this sector, which would involve dismantling both remaining tariffs as well as non-tariff barriers. Political commitment together with further analytical work in OECD and WTO should be able to concretise the double dividends for the economy and the environment which liberalisation offers here.

Such pressures are likely to be more acute where countries share a border and are characterised by large differences in income levels and regulatory regimes (particularly in terms of resources devoted to their enforcement). Still, the main problem with examples of this type, which often carry strong emotive appeal and

It is vital to focus on the rule, and not just the exceptions

attract considerable media attention, is that they typically represent exceptions, rather than the rule.

Empirical research devoted to pollution havens suggests that, in fact, the risk of redeployment of productive resources towards low-standard countries should not be overstated.[9] Several factors help explain this:

- Close to three quarters of global FDI flows originate in and are directed towards industrialised countries and are therefore subject to the more stringent environmental controls which typically apply in OECD countries.

■ Most FDI in pollution-intensive activities originating in industrialised countries heads for other developed economies, rather than to developing ones. The amount of FDI in pollution-intensive

industries in developing countries is actually *lower* as a share of total FDI inflows today than it was in 1972.[10]

■ Over 60 per cent of FDI flows take place in the less environmentally-intensive service industries. The projected rise in the share of services-related FDI world-wide should, therefore, result in a lessening of global environmental pressures.

■ While FDI in resource-based activities (e.g. mining) is generally more susceptible to differences in environmental costs, this type of FDI accounts for only a small share of total FDI directed towards serving local or regional export markets, both of which are considerably less sensitive to environmental costs.

■ Very few companies investing overseas seek to reduce environmental compliance costs as their primary goal. Operating costs (including environmental costs) are only one of several factors in location decisions and the costs of adhering to environmental regulations are typically a small part of total production costs for most firms. Surveys cite other factors, such as political risks, the size and growth potential of markets and the quality of infrastructure, as more important determinants of the locational decisions of firms.[11]

■ Surveys show that companies generally seek consistent environmental enforcement rather than lax enforcement and that they are usually willing to make new investments to improve the environment if their competitors, domestic and foreign, must meet the same standards.[12]

■ Rather than being attracted by low levels of environmental protection, firms often find locational benefits from higher environmental standards, including via lower operating costs (e.g., improved worker productivity due to better health and quality of life; reduced risk of incurring clean-up costs for past environmental damage).[13]

Box 6.3

Promoting eco-efficiency through greater market openness

The development of global markets through trade and investment liberalisation involves greater economic activity and thus more use of materials and resources, both renewable and non-renewable. However, the productivity with which resources are used can be increased considerably using the cleanest resource-efficient technologies. Examples abound in which energy and material efficiencies have been at least quadrupled using existing and new technologies and production methods. If these efficiency gains turn out to be profitable, the transition to a better quality environment can occur within the bounds of open market competition. Indeed, there are indications that eco-efficiency — the addition of more value to goods and services using fewer resources and emitting less pollution — can be positively correlated with shareholder value, consumer demands and with economy-wide benefits more generally. A good example is provided by Dupont, the US chemicals group, that has set a "zero emissions" goal for its world-wide operations. "Zero emissions" were set not only (or primarily) as a result of regulatory pressures, but also because the company felt that it would be rewarded in the marketplace for achieving maximum levels of eco-efficiency. For the transition to eco-efficiency to be realised through market forces, however, market signals must be employed to encourage the use of the cleanest technologies, to ensure their broadest diffusion through open trade and investment, and to discourage pollution and the waste of resources.

- The bulk of international investment is undertaken by large multi-national enterprises (MNEs) that typically operate at the highest corporate standard of environmental performance world-wide rather than tailoring their production methods to the level of regulatory enforcement prevailing in host country markets.[14] For example, a recent survey of MNEs' environmental performance carried out by the United Nations found that larger firms are more likely to have well-established environmental management systems and better overall environmental performance.[15]

- MNEs have become far more sensitive to consumer boycott campaigns, triggered by actual or perceived environmental negligence.[16]

- FDI has been found to promote the adoption and speedier diffusion of environmentally-friendlier technologies, along with the better information, managerial know-how and training programmes that foreign investors often have at their disposal.[17]

- Much FDI directed towards non-OECD countries relates to privatisation. Privatised firms are typically better managed and more accountable, which tends to reduce waste and pollution.[18] Infrastructural improvements are particularly important for improving the business environment in host countries and reducing operational costs. These economy-wide benefits help to leverage greater capital inflows, with studies showing that each $1 invested in privatised infrastructures results in $2.4 of additional FDI.[19]

- Because the demand for environmental quality tends to increase with income, any formation of a "pollution haven" tends to be self-limiting in light of the countervailing pressures economic growth brings to bear on polluters. Seen in this light, pollution havens may be as "transient" as low-wage havens.

Taken together, these findings point to a positive relationship between investment liberalisation and environmental stewardship. They also explain why enquiries into pollution havens have, on the whole, unearthed very little evidence suggesting that high environmental standards exert strongly negative impacts on competitiveness. Evidence that countries explicitly lower their environmental standards and succeed in attracting new FDI in pollution-intensive activities is equally hard to come by.[20]

III. ADOPTING
A PRACTICAL PERSPECTIVE

The above discussion suggests that there is every reason to believe that more open trade and investment can play a vital role in helping societies shift resources and patterns of production and consumption in more sustainable directions while still contributing to economic growth. There is, similarly, much evidence to suggest that policies which dampen growth prospects world-wide are unlikely to help redress environmental degradation.

Policies that dampen growth are unlikely to help redress environment degradation

It may be noted also that market liberalisation, especially when conducted through multilateral auspices, serves a central transparency role in helping to achieve greater environmental integrity by bringing greater international scrutiny to bear on domestic practices whose environmental effects cross national borders. With major environmental issues such as global warming, deforestation or ozone depletion widely recognised as having world-wide implications, the past few years have seen greatly intensified international dialogue and co-

Cross-border environmental challenges call for dialogue and co-operation

operation on the environmental front. Dialogue and co-operation, rather than coercion, are the optimal ways to address environmental challenges that are transboundary in nature, be it by developing common standards, negotiating multilateral environmental agreements or nurturing greater understanding between the trade, investment and environmental policy communities. Such understanding is particularly important in instances where the promotion of environmental goals may require the adoption of measures that restrict trade or investment.

Trade and investment liberalisation can strongly complement and reinforce sound environmental policies. On the other hand, it is almost always a poor substitute for inadequate environmental policies. There also remains the risk that liberalisation can exacerbate environmental problems when environmental policies are poorly designed or weakly enforced. What is needed, therefore, is adoption of a suitably coherent and mutually reinforcing policy stance. It may be noted in this regard that harmonised environmental standards are not appropriate in situations where local environmental conditions or natural resource endowments justify differences in these standards. Where assimilative capacities differ, for example, efficiency requires that environmental standards reflect these differences. Harmonisation is most

Trade and investment liberalisation are a complement but not a substitute for inadequate environmental policies

appropriate in situations involving international externalities or spillover effects, and where the location of the pollution does not matter (e.g., climate change). However, despite their importance, such situations represent only a small proportion of all environmental problems. Indeed, most forms of environmental degradation remain predominantly local in origin and effect.

It is also well recognised that governments must have the right and the ability to address effectively environmental problems and to cooperate internationally to deal with environment problems of a transboundary, regional or global nature. Moreover, as outlined in the following chapter, there is nothing in existing international trade rules that fundamentally impairs the capacity of governments to deal with environmental protection within their respective territories. As OECD Member countries recently noted:

"The most frequent use of trade measures for environmental purposes is in conjunction with national product requirements i.e., requiring imports to meet environmental, safety and health requirements for products. Such regulations are clearly permitted under the current multilateral trade rules, subject to agreed disciplines."[21]

This study is not intended to describe all the more detailed issues that arise in the context of ongoing discussions aimed at ensuring that the interaction of trade, investment and environment policies are further enhanced. It can certainly be acknowledged that there are issues where future progress can and should be made. It is, however, a matter of maintaining an overall perspective on the scope of the agenda. At this point it seems a fair judgement that such a pragmatic and constructive approach is warranted rather than any need to step back from the fundamental direction in which both policy domains are currently working.

NOTES

1. See OECD (1994*a*) and OECD (1995*a*).

2. See Dasgupta, S., Mody, A. and Sinha, S.(1995*)*; Lucas, R., Wheeler, D. and Heitige, H. (1992); and Seldon, T.M. and Song, D. (1994).

3. See Dasgupta, S. *et al* (1995).

4. See OECD (1997*b*), *op cit*.

5. See Lucas, R., Wheeler, D. and Hettige, H. (1992), *op.cit.*

6. On the other hand, liberalisation could also make environmentally-harmful products (e.g., hazardous substances) or technologies more accessible, but the risk here seems small, given that these products do not represent a very large part of total international trade, nor are they necessarily the most serious source of environmental problems in the first place.

7. See Johnstone, N. (1997).

8. See Birdsall, N. and Wheeler, D. (1993), and Lucas, Wheeler and Hettige (1992).

9. See Low, P. and Yeats, A. (1992); Blazeiczak, J. (1993); and Grossman, G. and Krueger, A.B. (1992).

10. See Sorsa, P. (1994).

11. See Gentry, B.S. *et al.* (1996).

12. See Esty, D.C. and Gentry, B.S. in OECD (1997*j*).

13. See Barrett, S. (1993) and Schmidheiny, S. and Business Council for Sustainable Development (1992).

14. See Schmidheiny, S. and Business Council for Sustaintable Development (1992), *op.cit.*

15. See UNCTAD (1994).

16. See Garrod, B. (1997).

17. See Johnstone, N. (1997).

18. See Gentry, B.S. *et al* (1996), *op.cit.*

19. See International Finance Corporation (1997).

20. See Mani, M. and Wheeler, D. (1997); Birdsall, N. and Wheeler, D. (1993), *op.cit.* See also Adams, J. (1997).

21. See OECD (1995*a*).

MARKET OPENNESS AND NATIONAL SOVEREIGNTY

G iven that globalisation trends are often described as "creating a borderless world", it is not surprising that there is a national sovereignty dimension to public concerns about the pace and scope of globalisation and liberalisation. Sovereignty concerns also feature prominently in public scrutiny of specific trade and investment agreements, particularly by those concerned about environmental, consumer safety, social equity and cultural diversity issues. These concerns tend to relate to the perception that increased global competition, underpinned by global trade and investment agreements, is eroding the capacity of governments to exercise national "regulatory" sovereignty. That is, to independently determine national policy objectives and implement regulatory decisions on both economic and social issues. This section focuses on the implications of liberalisation for national policy and regulatory sovereignty and the rationale for multilateral rules-based systems in the trade and investment fields.[1]

Sovereignty concerns arise from globalisation ...

Sovereignty issues have, of course, long been an important aspect of international relations. In recent decades, as the world has become significantly more interdependent in both security and economic terms, sovereign governments have invested considerable effort in the negotiation of international agreements – in arms control, security co-operation, trade

and investment liberalisation, environmental protection and a host of other issues. The fundamental reason for doing so is to bind other countries to mutually beneficial sets of rules that aim to promote civilised international behaviour in such areas. Such agreements, in effect, represent the consensus of sovereign Member countries about what should and can be achieved through *concerted* action on the matters covered by an agreement. Multilateral treaties thus embody a co-operative approach by sovereign governments to the challenges of interdependence.

... and from the operation of multilateral treaties

It is also worth bearing in mind that sovereignty is a deeply subjective and relative concept, for both individual citizens and societies. Furthermore, much of the campaigning by those concerned about the operation of international trade and investment agreements is conducted through mass media, the Internet and the lobbying of governments. It is thus difficult to gauge the extent to which such concerns about the sovereignty-impairment effects of trade and investment liberalisation are shared in wider public opinion. Moreover, specific sovereignty concerns arising from international trade and investment agreements

These concerns differ among citizens and across societies ...

or institutions are not necessarily homogeneous among OECD Member countries, nor within non-OECD countries. While all OECD Member countries belong to the WTO, the IMF and the World Bank, some are also members, or aspiring members, of the European Single Market; and most, but not all, of the others belong to free trade agreements with immediate neighbours.[2]

That being said, sovereignty concerns clearly do form part of both the broad political culture and the decision-making context for trade and investment liberalisation in a number of OECD countries. There is no doubt that many citizens in OECD countries are concerned about the impact of globalisation and the dizzying pace of change, and that such issues influence their views on the role of governments as well as the way they vote. No doubt too, many citizens could nominate at least a couple of specific "local" examples of national trade and investment liberalisation decisions or international trade and investment rules that affront their sense of national sovereignty, such as a factory closure or a WTO dispute ruling against their country.

... but have some common themes

I. LIBERALISATION AND NATIONAL POLICY FLEXIBILITY AND SOVEREIGNTY

It bears emphasising that governments generally undertake trade and investment liberalisation as part of overall national economic reform strategies aimed at maximising the welfare of their citizens. Indeed, for most governments liberalisation is a means to important ends, whereby improved international competitiveness may actually increase a country's room to manoeuvre on domestic economic and social policies by improving its national income and making it less vulnerable to external shocks. In this way, key aspects of sovereignty may be seen as strengthened rather than diluted, albeit in the context of an undeniably interdependent and rapidly changing world. The challenge remains to convincingly present liberalisation strategies and decisions as reinforcing sustainable economic growth to the wider benefit of societies, rather than as ends in themselves.

Liberalisation strategies can enhance sovereignty and policy flexibility ...

Moreover, liberalisation is almost never "imposed" on countries, by other countries. Rather, through international liberalisation negotiations, governments seek to establish the rules by which the participants agree to play in the future. In such negotiations, as at other international events, democratic governments represent their citizens. Most, if not all, OECD countries have established extensive consultative and information-sharing procedures for input to such negotiations by all interested domestic parties, and national Parliaments remain the ultimate place for deliberation and decision-making on treaty acceptance.

... and multilateral treaties represent the exercise of sovereignty rather than its surrender

Furthermore, market liberalisation does not involve the wholesale dismantling of domestic regulatory measures. On the contrary, liberalised markets rely on effective and efficient domestic regulation to maintain public standards or protect public interests in a large number of areas, including *inter alia*, customs inspection, clearance and control, product quality and safety assurance systems, environmental quality and protection and the prudential oversight of banking and finance. (See Appendix B) Indeed, the recent financial

Liberalisation and effective regulation go hand-in-hand ...

market turmoil experienced by a number of Asian economies is in part a reminder that a sound regulatory framework for financial market supervision is an essential complement to market liberalisation. However, while liberalisation decisions often need to be supplemented by domestic regulatory reforms to improve the efficiency and transparency of market functions and the quality of regulatory performance therein, this is a matter for national decision-making rather than something that is directed or imposed externally.

In fact, notwithstanding their achievements in trade and investment liberalisation and the negotiation of a large number of international agreements at the bilateral, regional, plurilateral or multilateral level, OECD countries exhibit a striking diversity of economic and social policies and regulatory frameworks, with wide variations amongst them in, *inter alia*, tax and public expenditure shares in GDP, corporate tax rates, the level of the minimum wage and employee/employer bargaining systems, social security systems, competition and other commercial regulatory frameworks, building standards, retail and distribution systems, environmental protection programmes, and cultural protection and promotion schemes.

... and market economies exhibit great diversity in regulatory approaches

For their part, multilateral trade and investment agreements do not aim to put into question *objectives* of national policies or regulations, whether on trade, investment or any other matters. Nor do they regard all measures to implement them as *a priori* simply unnecessary barriers to doing global business (see Boxes 7.1 and 7.3 - 7.5 on the WTO and Box 7.2 on the MAI). For example, to complement market access liberalisation in agricultural and food products, an agreement on sanitary and phytosanitary measures (e.g. quarantine and food safety measures) was agreed in the Uruguay Round. This agreement recognises that there are important and legitimate human, animal and plant health and safety policy considerations that bear protecting, including through restrictions on international trade. In this instance, there was a consensus among GATT Members that such an agreement was a good idea.

Multilateral agreements respect regulatory objectives

On the other hand, in the absence of such a consensus, an issue with international trade dimensions such as broadcasting was not a subject of multilateral trade liberalisation or rule-making in the Uruguay Round. Nor are countries inhibited under WTO rules from providing financial assistance to their artistic communities. Those situations have not prevented, of course, the evident increasing commercial exchange of cultural activity and material as a consumer-driven phenomenon in, for example, the tourism, music and film sectors. It is simply that there was not a consensus to consolidate this liberalisation in the form of an intergovernmental trade agreement.

II. THE RATIONALE FOR MULTILATERAL TRADE AND INVESTMENT RULES

Multilateral treaties are based on recognition by participating countries of the value of voluntary acceptance of, and adherence to, a common set of rules for the issues covered by the treaty. Through such treaties, governments, in effect, agree to act in concert to maximise the achievement of common goals or the development of solutions to shared problems. In doing so, governments use multilateral frameworks to share the burden and maximise the possible benefits for their countries of achieving goals or solving problems at the international level.

The essence of multilateralism is co-operation and concerted action ...

The WTO and its predecessor the GATT were founded on recognition of the fundamental importance of this approach to international trade. In effect, the multilateral trading system provides rules for the orderly conduct of an open world trading system which, whether in the aftermath of the Great Depression and the Second World War, or in today's context of globalisation and deepening economic integration, are vital concepts for the stable functioning of international civil society. The proposed MAI aims to apply the same approach to international investment, codifying the best practices embedded in existing bilateral and regional investment treaties. In 1996-97, one such agreement was concluded every two days. This suggests that there is reciprocal interest in home and host countries alike for placing investment relations on a fairer, more secure and predictable footing.

... to promote stability and order in open global markets

Trade and investment agreements are based on the shared premise of their members that international trade and investment makes a vital contribution to the growth and development of their economies and to employment opportunities within them. And the actual experience of countries participating in liberalising trade and investment agreement in the post-war period has confirmed this. Furthermore, as signatories are invariably importers and exporters of goods, services, ideas and capital, the rules they negotiate represent a balance between their interests in securing and improving market access into other countries, and their need for competitively-priced imports and for technology-diffusing, productivity-enhancing

Members share a vital interest in having each other adhere to the same rules ...

and employment-creating inflows of foreign direct investment. Thus the rules of the WTO now, and those being negotiated for the MAI, are based on the mutual interest of participating governments in having each other curtail the use of the most trade or investment-restrictive measures, and abide by the same rules for the use of other measures.

Nevertheless, the WTO is *not*, and nor would the MAI be, an agreement to eliminate all trade and investment barriers *per se*. Rather, multilateral liberalisation tends to be incremental in nature and scope, involving periodic reviews and negotiations to keep both the rules and the openness of international markets up to date, *on a multilaterally-agreed basis*. Thus, it took almost fifty years, and eight painstaking "rounds" of multilateral negotiations, to achieve the reduction by GATT Members of non-discriminatory tariffs on manufacturing goods from the average of 40 per cent that prevailed in 1948 to the less than 4 per cent average that will prevail when most Uruguay Round commitments are implemented by 2000. Furthermore, reviews of the implementation and operation of most of the WTO agreements are scheduled for the period 1997-2000; and negotiations on further multilateral liberalisation of services and agriculture are only due to resume by 2000, seven years after the conclusion of the Uruguay Round agreements on those issues.

... and to liberalise on a progressive, non-discriminatory basis

It is also noteworthy that, while the Uruguay Round was the most comprehensive multilateral trade negotiating round ever achieved, many of its results reflected actions by OECD Members that had already commenced autonomously or in a regional context during the course of the

Multilateral liberalisation reflects sovereign decisions to do so

Round (see Box 7.1).[3] These examples demonstrate the fact that governments' participation in multilateral trade and investment negotiations constitutes the actual exercise of their sovereignty rather than any surrender of it; and that the negotiating process accordingly reflects the need for Member governments to move forward in a way that is consistent with their domestic political and constitutional frameworks.

Moreover, there is clear recognition on the part of governments of the importance of assuring that the agreements they enter, not only explicitly recognise and protect their ability to establish domestic regulatory or social policy objectives, but also that they guard against an unintended weakening of that ability, including, in the area of dispute settlement. That is why MAI negotiators have focused a good deal of attention on this aspect of that proposed treaty. Although it is currently being negotiated, in the interests of transparency, a summary of the main features of the proposed MAI is included in Box 7.2.

Multilateral agreements explicitly protect sovereign objectives in a number of areas

---

Box 7.1

The Uruguay Round and national sovereignty in OECD countries

Actual trade and investment liberalisation undertaken by national governments continues to run some way ahead of that which is committed to or "bound" under the WTO framework. Although the Uruguay Round was, in numbers of participants and the scope and value of world trade covered, the biggest multilateral trade negotiation ever conducted, its implementation and the creation of the WTO was far from being a wholesale "surrender of national sovereignty". On the contrary, the object, purpose and achievement of the Round was an actual strengthening of participant governments' national economies with the attendant increased freedom of choice that is at the core of the exercise of sovereignty.

Most of the changes to OECD countries' national laws, regulations and practices to implement the new agreements on issues such as anti-dumping, intellectual property, product standards, licensing of imports and professional service providers, were at the level of detail rather than first principles. This was because the new WTO rules on these issues were either an evolution in existing GATT Codes or codified in general terms the prevailing direction of reforms on these issues by OECD countries. Nevertheless, by doing so, the new agreements greatly enhanced the security, predictability and transparency of international trade.

Similarly, most of the liberalisation commitments made by OECD countries in the services area were in the nature of WTO bindings of national reforms already in place, the great bulk of which were enacted during the course of the Uruguay Round. And the agriculture subsidy reduction commitments of the US and EU reflected the terms of the domestic and bilateral agreements they reached on such practices. For a number of OECD countries, the implementation of agriculture market access commitments did require reform arising from the conversion of non-tariff barriers to tariffs[4]. On manufacturing tariffs, some OECD countries such as Australia and New Zealand, essentially bound the significant autonomous tariff reductions they had undertaken in the previous decade; while others made cuts of around one-third to already quite low prevailing tariff levels.

By contrast, many developing countries had to introduce significant new laws or amendments to existing ones to implement the Uruguay Round Single Undertaking, particularly in services, intellectual property, product standards and anti-dumping. Developing countries also started further behind in liberalising basic market access conditions in their markets. This explains why developing countries were granted longer implementation periods than OECD countries for most of these issues.

III. COVERAGE OF MULTILATERAL TRADE AND INVESTMENT AGREEMENTS

As already noted, sovereignty concerns about trade and investment liberalisation and the operation of multilateral agreements are far from homogeneous. Some concerns, of course, continue to arise primarily from the multilateral agreement of governments to limit their recourse to specific trade and investment measures, or the use of trade or investment

Concerns about liberalisation "overriding" other objectives need to be addressed

sanctions. However, a broader range of concerns are also evident, such as that trade and investment agreements and their dispute settlement processes increasingly exercise an "override" capacity with respect to other national regulatory domains, in particular with regard to the environment, food safety, cultural diversity and social cohesion.

Thus, it is crucial to improve public understanding of the purpose and coverage of multilateral trade and investment rules. This is particularly so in regard to multilateral requirements of non-discriminatory treatment of domestic and foreign products, and their extension to services and investments, which

---

Box 7.2

The Multilateral Agreement on Investment (MAI)

International investment has become increasingly important as a vehicle for economic integration. Yet, unlike trade, the multilateral system lacks a comprehensive framework for investment. The MAI currently under negotiation in the OECD will consolidate and build on the existing OECD instruments covering investment. It will also complement the work of other multilateral rule-making bodies, notably the World Trade Organization and the International Monetary Fund.

The MAI will address investors and investments, including their establishment, expansion, operation and sale. Investment will be defined broadly to include enterprises, real estate, portfolio investments, other financial instruments and intangible assets. The MAI aims to establish a uniform high standard of investor protection with an effective system for resolving investment disputes. It is also designed to secure the investment liberalisation already achieved and to provide a platform for future negotiations. By achieving these goals, the MAI will promote economic growth and efficiency. It will help reduce the risks of international business by providing predictability and security for international investors and their investments.

Launched in May 1995, the negotiations on the MAI aimed to develop a free standing international treaty open to all OECD Members and the European Community and to accession by non-Members willing and able to meet its obligations. Five non-Members presently attend the negotiations as observers. In addition, there has been extensive dialogue with non-Member countries, with business and labour and with non-governmental organisations.

Core MAI Disciplines:

■ Transparency: publication of laws and regulations affecting investments.

■ National Treatment: foreign investors and investments to be treated no less favourably than domestic investors and investments.

■ Most Favoured Nation Treatment: investors and investments from one MAI Party to be treated no less favourably than investors from another MAI Party.

■ Transfer of Funds: investment-related payments, including capital, profits and dividends, must be freely permitted to and from the host country;

(continued on following page)

are seen by some concerned observers as preventing governments from regulating domestically to uphold national standards and values. Therefore, Box 7.3 presents in summary form the national measures subject to the WTO rules, as well as the principal requirements and exceptions for such measures. In addition, and importantly for purposes of a discussion of sovereignty concerns, Box 7.4 presents in summary form what the WTO rules do not require.

Notwithstanding the recognition of the co-existence of a range of public policy objectives, and provision of exceptions for them, in, for example, the WTO and present efforts to do so

in the MAI, public concerns about "regulatory override" appears related at least in part to the more comprehensive and binding nature of multilateral rules and dispute settlement processes for trade and investment, compared to those for some non-economic issues. This reflects, in part, the fact that multilateral co-operation on commercial issues has been developed over several decades. Nevertheless, it is worth noting that

The issue is more about improving complementarity between liberalisation and other objectives

---

Box 7.2 (continued)

■ Entry and Stay of Key Personnel: investors and key personnel, such as senior managers or specialised technicians, should be granted permission to enter and stay temporarily to work in support of MAI investments.

■ Performance Requirements: prohibitions on certain requirements imposed on investors, such as minimum export targets for goods and services, local content rules or technology transfer requirements.

■ Expropriation: may only be undertaken for a public purpose, with prompt, adequate and effective compensation.

■ Dispute Settlement: provision for resolving disputes through consultations, with recourse to binding arbitration of disputes between states and between foreign investors and host states, if necessary.

Furthermore, the MAI disciplines:

■ should be fully compatible with the pursuit of high labour and environmental standards. There is agreement among MAI negotiators that the agreement should not infringe on normal regulatory powers of governments which are exercised in a non-discriminatory manner and in accordance with accepted international norms. Preambular language, provisions in the text of

the agreement, and association to the MAI of the OECD Guidelines for Multinational Enterprises (with their chapters on employment and industrial relations and on the environment) are under consideration.

However, the MAI:

■ will not eliminate all barriers to foreign investment. Any country will be able to take measures necessary to protect its national security or to ensure the integrity and stability of its financial system. Temporary safeguard provisions will enable countries to take measures necessary to respond to a balance of payments crisis. Country-specific exceptions, negotiated among MAI Parties, will permit each country to maintain non-conforming laws and regulations;

■ will not mandate detailed domestic measures affecting investment, nor require Member countries to adopt a uniform set of investment regulations;

■ will not prevent Parties from providing funds for domestic policy purposes; and

■ will not require Parties to accept each others' product or service quality or safety standards.

Box 7.3

Areas of national policy subject to WTO rules

The WTO rules cover national measures used to regulate trade in goods and services, and national systems for the protection of trade-related intellectual property rights.

For goods, this includes (since 1948) border measures such as tariffs and other duties, anti-dumping and countervailing duties, import quotas and bans; non-tariff measures such as customs fees and valuation procedures, rules of origin, subsidies; and internal measures that apply to imported products inside national borders, such as taxes, charges and regulations that affect a product's competitiveness in the domestic market.

For services, this includes (since 1995) national measures affecting trade in services, such as laws and regulations pertaining to the provision of services across national borders or through commercial presence of foreign service suppliers within national borders (e.g., through temporary entry of persons or via investment), the regulation of purchase, payment or use of services, and access to or use of required public services.

Core WTO rules:

■ Publication and transparent administration of trade-related border and internal measures.

■ Non-discriminatory application of measures affecting foreign products and services (so-called most-favoured nation, or MFN, treatment).

■ Non-discriminatory application of internal measures affecting market regulation for goods and services to both foreign and domestically-produced products and services (national treatment and MFN).

■ However, exceptions to most-favoured-nation (MFN) treatment are permitted for regional integration agreements (i.e. free trade areas and customs unions); reservations to MFN and national treatment for traded services are permitted; and tariffs may be applied to imports only. Exceptions to MFN, national treatment or other WTO rules may be taken for measures which relate to a legitimate national or international public policy objective, under the general and security exceptions clauses of WTO Agreements (see Box 7.5). Other exceptions are available to deal with sudden and serious balance-of-payments problems or sudden import surges which cause serious injury to domestic industry.

■ Maintenance of country schedules showing binding ceiling levels for tariffs; binding ceilings on subsidy outlays for agriculture; and, for services, national laws and regulations limiting market access or non-discriminatory treatment of foreign firms.

■ Requirements not to use internal regulatory measures to undermine scheduled market access commitments or, if this is unavoidable, to undertake consultations with principally affected trading partners to negotiate compensation.

■ Some other rules for national administration of covered measures, e.g., licensing of imported goods or foreign services professionals, anti-dumping investigations, development of product standards.

■ Adherence to multilateral rules and procedures for the resolution of disputes arising from matters covered by these rules.

■ Principal proscribed measures are export subsidies for manfactured products, import quotas for manufactured and agricultural products, and import bans.

many of those concerned to protect non-economic values being "overridden" by market access and non-discrimination commitments in international trade and investment negotiations, do not oppose such inter-governmental treaty-making *per se*. Rather, they want market access-related agreements to include more specific standards or safeguards to uphold non-market access values. In these terms, the debate is actually less about loss of sovereignty than about seeking to create greater consistency or balance between the open global market place and international efforts on non-economic priorities.

To the extent this is so, it is clearly a matter to be resolved by efforts to enhance the complementarity of such policy domains rather than retreating from the exercise of international treaty-making itself. While beyond the scope of this particular study, that challenge is, indeed, at the heart of the multilateral agenda already in such areas as, for example, trade and the environment, and will clearly remain so for the foreseeable future.

IV. THE WTO AND NATIONAL POLICY SOVEREIGNTY

(a) Non-discrimination and regulatory sovereignty

Non-discrimination rules do not operate to inhibit national governments' capacity to maintain high national standards, for example, in protecting the environment, ensuring food safety or the safety and rights of workers. Rather, the requirement to treat foreign goods, services or firms like domestic ones means that national regulatory standards for goods and services that are supplied by foreign trade and/or investment as well as by domestic firms, need to be designed to maintain an equality of competitive opportunities between foreign and

---

Box 7.4

What the WTO rules do not require

■ Do not prevent define or seek to curtail Member countries from establishing their own trade or non-trade policy objectives, or prevent Member countries from applying regulatory measures necessary to achieve those objectives.

■ Do not require Member countries to eliminate all barriers to imports of goods or services.

■ Do not direct in detail, national administrative or procedural systems for the use of trade measures, nor require Member countries to adopt a uniform set of trade regulations.

■ Do not require Member countries to reduce tariffs or barriers to foreign services firms – rather, it provides a multilateral forum for negotiation of reductions, and a mechanism for binding them to provide predictability and security of market access, where there is a freely arrived at agreement to do so.

■ Do not prevent Member countries from providing public funds for a broad range of domestic policy and regulatory reasons (see Box 7.6).

■ Do not require Member countries to accept each others' product or service quality or safety standards. Rather, the WTO provides rules for national products standards, including criteria for the preparation, adoption and application by each country measures used to fulfil its legitimate objectives. It also encourages, without mandating, regulatory co-operation aimed at the international harmonisation of standards or the development of mutual recognition agreements.

---

domestic participants in the national market. As exporters, all countries have a vital stake in the maintenance and integrity of this basic principle.

This means that countries' economic and social regulatory standards can be as high or stringent as desired, but *they must not be made even higher* for foreign participants in the national market. There is, of course, *no* requirement for such regulatory standards to be lower for foreign firms than for domestic ones. The WTO also provides (as would the proposed MAI) a number of general and specific exceptions to non-discrimination and other rules for measures relating to the achievement of a defined public policy objective (see Box 7.5). By agreement of WTO Members, recourse to these exceptions is subject to overall requirements that the achievement of such an objective through an otherwise WTO-inconsistent trade restriction should not be accomplished by *arbitrary or unjustified* discrimination, or as a disguised restriction on trade.

The guiding philosophy of this approach is to discourage the resort to discrimination, particularly for disguised protectionist reasons, that characterised the breakdown of the international trading system between the two World Wars. If it can be demonstrated – and it has yet to be – that a legitimate national policy objective cannot be achieved except through discriminatory trade measures, multilateral trade agreements such as the WTO would not prevent that.

All countries have a vital interest in the basic principles of "fair play" – non-discrimination and national treatment

The maintenance of open markets is itself an extremely important public policy objective; and the essence of multilateral trade co-operation is that governments have agreed to avoid unnecessarily trade-restrictive measures in achieving their policy objectives. In practical terms, unnecessary trade-restrictiveness is avoided through adherence to the agreed multilateral rules for the measure in question, in particular in relation to transparent and impartial preparation, implementation and administration of such measures, including prior notification and consultation with affected trading partners.

(b) The WTO and the protection of domestic industries and jobs

The WTO rules do *not* prohibit the protection of domestic industry *per se*, but they do, however, require that this be done in a transparent and non-discriminatory way. In the case of goods, this is principally through the tariff, and for services through the right to schedule limitations on market access and on affording foreign firms the same rights as domestic ones. WTO rules also permit countries to temporarily increase tariff protection for specific products to provide a "safeguard" against unexpected import surges that, while they are not unfair or illegal under WTO rules, have an adverse effect on local firms. These temporary safeguards permit a government to increase protection for a limited time while the domestic industry adjusts to the import competition.

WTO rules do not prohibit all measures to protect domestic jobs and industries

In 1983, the US-based Harley-Davidson motorcycle and classic engineering company applied for and received such safeguard

---

Box 7.5

Illustrative list of national public policy objectives recognised by the WTO multilateral trade agreements*

■ Protection of human life and health, and the environment.

■ Product and service quality and safety.

■ Control of plant and animal diseases.

■ The need for prudential regulation to ensure the integrity and stability of financial systems.

■ Protection of archaeological treasures.

■ Maintenance of public order.

■ Prevention of fraud.

■ National security reasons.

* Drawn from GATT Articles XX and XXI, GATS Articles XIV and XV and TRIPS Article 73.

protection from a surge in imported motorcycles. This gave the company time to adjust and increase its competitiveness and, in fact, Harley-Davidson asked the US Government to remove the safeguard protection ahead of schedule in recognition of it having adjusted to the import competition. WTO negotiations on a similar clause for services are underway. The use of other measures to regulate imported goods, such as anti-dumping measures, food safety standards and product quality and safety standards, are supposed to be used for those specific purposes – to counter injury to local industry from unfair pricing conduct by foreign competitors, and to uphold product safety and quality, respectively, and not for industry protection purposes.

Nor do WTO rules prevent governments from directing public funds to subsidies or other payments for structural or trade adjustment assistance, either to firms or dis-placed workers, so long as such payments are not used for ongoing subsidisation of production or exports. The WTO's prohibition on export subsidies and export incentive schemes for manufacturing industries is based on the mutual self-interest of Members in preventing ruinous subsidy competition of the type encountered in agriculture. The latter became a major source of international trade distortion and dispute; before proving to be beyond even the biggest countries' budgetary means, as well as being an inequitable social distribution of public funds. Agriculture export subsidies will be a focus of future WTO negotiating rounds.

Some types of subsidies are permitted ...

The WTO rules do, however, permit (and exempt from countervailing action by trading partners) a range of domestic subsidies, as set out in Box 7.6. An even broader range are permissible in themselves, and the rules simply provide that where some of these have

... and public funds may be used for structural or trade adjustment schemes if governments wish to do so

injurious effects on other trading partners, those countries are entitled to exercise their own sovereignty to take counter-measures accordingly. Thus, the WTO rules provide scope for Member governments to protect domestic industry from international compe-tition on a short or longer-term basis, if they wish to do so.

(c) Maintaining regulatory sovereignty over the way products are produced

As noted above, trade and investment agreements do not put into question, the right of countries to set their policy objectives in such areas as environmental protection or the health and safety of citizens. When it comes to application of implementing measures they have considerable freedom to use restrictions for environmental protection or resource conservation within their territory – as long as they do not apply a double standard – i.e., they do not use the restriction in a discriminatory way vis-à-vis other countries and they avoid unnecessary trade- or investment-restrictiveness (as already noted, in practice this means adhering to the agreed rules for use of measures that restrict trade). It is true that under the multilateral trade rules, countries cannot apply differential measures based on the process and production methods used in another country to make their goods. But the reason for that is itself all about respecting sovereignty – the sovereign right of each country to regulate its own process and production methods and to not have them imposed from abroad.

V. DISPUTE SETTLEMENT AND TRADE SANCTIONS

The WTO is not, nor can it become, some kind of supra-national busybody that will impose its predetermined values and standards on national governments or communities. The WTO is not an independent entity and its Secretariat acts solely in the service of the membership in the conduct of WTO business.

Multilateral trade dispute settlement is conducted between sovereign governments ...

All WTO disputes are brought by WTO Member governments. Under the WTO dispute settlement procedures, Members exercise due restraint in bringing disputes, having first utilised consultative approaches to seek mutually satisfactory solutions. Such dispute panels as are established, and the appellate body proceedings which may follow a panel's conclusions, are subject to a code of conduct developed and adopted by the WTO Member countries. WTO dispute proceedings are conducted at inter-governmental level and, thus, in private (just as nearly all internal deliberations of Member governments are). Nevertheless, transparency measures have been introduced and are reviewed regularly.

Moreover, the basis for the conclusions reached by panels in any such disputes is purely and simply the rules that each and every sovereign government has itself freely chosen to abide by. The Appellate Body exists to review the legal basis of panel conclusions in accordance with the principles of public international law. As noted earlier, the rules of the WTO provide wide scope for retention of national regulatory differences. Such differences, and the national policy objectives underlying them,

... according to rules and procedures agreed by sovereign governments

are not *per se* the subject of dispute settlement scrutiny, but rather, whether the measures themselves are discriminatory, or in other ways breach the agreed multilateral trade rules.

Thus, to the extent that domestic regulations are challenged by another WTO Member, and thus come before a WTO panel, it is because it is claimed, by another WTO Member, that the preparation, implementation or administration of the measure results in unnecessary restriction on international trade or other breach of commitments under the WTO. It is only these aspects which are examined in the dispute settlement process. It should also be borne in mind that the objective is *dispute settlement*, on mutually satisfactory terms; and not regulatory interference.

Panel conclusions are put before the membership for adoption, which occurs unless there is a consensus not to do so. Under the GATT, panel conclusions were often blocked indefinitely by the losing party. The additional innovation of the appellate body in the WTO dispute settlement process was intended to provide greater consistency and accuracy in rulings by following the appellate models of domestic courts. Nor does the WTO have any kind of supra-national status to compel any of its Members to adhere to its provisions. It is essentially a framework for Agreements reached by the Members themselves.

Thus if a country is found by a WTO dispute panel, confirmed by the appellate body, to have violated one of its obligations, that country retains the sovereign right to determine its response to the finding, by developing its own plan for remedying the breach of its obligations. Of course, every sovereign government knows that – as with any contract – the system's durability and benefits depend on all the Member countries continuing to abide by their commitments, including respecting the conclusions of an independent panel as to whether these have been breached. It is as much an exercise of sovereignty to abide by the rules following a dispute settlement case, as it was to have agreed to the rules in the first place. And the mutual benefits which motivate sovereign governments in negotiating the rules in the first place remain as much of a motivation for implementation of dispute settlement recommendations to bring themselves into conformity with the rules.

Conformity with WTO rules and decisions cannot be compelled by any external force against a sovereign government's will. However, should such a country refuse to abide by its commitments altogether, the WTO rules permit the country that had originally brought the dispute to withdraw a concession of equivalent commercial value which it had previously negotiated with that country. This is intended as a procedure of last resort, and has not been utilised under the WTO system. Nevertheless, it underlines the point that the exercise of sovereignty has been built into the dispute settlement process from the outset. It also bears recalling that where no agreed rules exist, the WTO dispute settlement procedures have no role to play: they cannot and do not invent new rules and force them on WTO signatories.

Multilateral dispute settlement can only interpret existing commitments; it cannot create new obligations

With regard to the use of trade sanctions, as already noted, trade and investment agreements aim to prevent the use of the most trade-distorting measures, such as import or foreign investment bans, except when alternative, less restrictive measures to achieve a legitimate national or international policy objective are not available or adequate for the purpose. However, it is sometimes proposed that these conditions should be waived, and recourse to trade measures permitted, to enforce adherence by some countries to certain environmental or human rights standards.

Certain exceptions are permitted in particular defined circumstances

As noted above, trade agreements do not prevent their Members from maintaining or introducing measures to regulate imports into their own territories, as long as these are in conformity with agreed rules, such as

---

Box 7.6

Illustrative list of subsidies permitted under WTO rules

Manufacturing (provided such subsidies are decoupled from production or export outputs)

- "generally available" subsidies (i.e., subsidies not targeted at specific firms or industries)

- R & D activities

- assistance to disadvantaged regions with high long-term unemployment or depressed income per capita or household incomes

- assistance to promote adaptation to new environmental laws or regulations

Agriculture

- provision of rural advisory and research programmes

- pest and disease control, marketing and promotion services

- income support to farmers that is decoupled from production performance

- government contributions to farmers' income insurance and income safety-net programmes, structural adjustment assistance through producer or resource retirement programmes

- payments under environmental and disadvantaged region programmes

- WTO rules on subsidies for services industries are the object of ongoing negotiations

---

transparency, non-discriminatory application, non-arbitrariness and that they are not unnecessarily restrictive. This includes regulation of imports on the basis that the processing or production methods used to make a particular product pose health risks or cause damage to the environment of the importing Member, subject to adherence to agreed rules about notification and transparency in the introduction and administration of such measures. However, trade agreements draw the line at measures which seek to impose such national standards unilaterally or extra-territorially on other Members, including through trade sanctions of either a specific or general nature. This is because the primary role of trade or investment agreements in good international governance and civil society is to maintain the transparency and predictability of open markets for trade in goods and services.

Agreements such as the WTO, or the prospective MAI, have not, in fact, inhibited signatories from playing a full part in inter-national treaty-making on environmental and human rights issues; nor have they stood in the way of the use of international trade bans in those or other instances, where an international consensus to do so is reached, for example, in the case of environmental treaties such as the Montreal Protocol (ozone depletion), CITES (trade in endangered species), and the Basel Convention (transport of hazardous materials); or in the case of trade sanctions taken against certain countries in accordance with UN Security Council resolutions.

NOTES

1. For a fuller discussion of linkages between international institutions and sovereign state behaviour, see Keohane (1998).

2. For example: the United States, Canada and Mexico are parties to NAFTA; Australia and New Zealand to ANZCERTA; Poland, Hungary and the Czech Republic to CEFTA; and Switzerland, Norway and Iceland to EFTA. There is an FTA between EFTA and the EU; Turkey has an FTA with EFTA and a customs union with the EU. Japan and Korea are the only OECD member countries not also party to a free trade agreement, although they are members of APEC, as are the US, Canada, Mexico, Australia, New Zealand and several non-OECD member economies.

3. A particularly vivid non-trade example of the *ex post* multilateralisation of reformist national decisions is the Comprehensive Test Ban Treaty, which was concluded in late 1995, once the world's major nuclear powers had agreed to renounce nuclear testing because they no longer needed to perform such tests. While some might argue about the present-value merits of such a treaty, it reduces the prospects in the future that countries will revert to potentially destructive and destabilising behaviour.

4. However, it is important to bear in mind that the impending Uruguay Round deadline, and the call to resume agricultural trade negotiations by the year 2000 as part of the WTO's so-called "built-in agenda" are factors providing impetus to fundamental reforms in agricultural policies worldwide.

THE WAY FORWARD: STRENGTHENING PUBLIC SUPPORT FOR TRADE AND INVESTMENT LIBERALISATION

The premise of this study is that market openness brings benefits for our countries and citizens. That being so, there is a strong case for proponents of market openness to devote more time and effort in explaining to citizens and their representatives what those benefits are, and how trade and investment liberalisation makes a vital contribution to prosperity. Efforts must also be made to explain how legitimate concerns over adverse labour market developments, particularly for unskilled workers, or over instances of environmental degradation are almost always certain to be compounded by protectionist responses and are typically best addressed through other (non-trade or investment) policy instruments.

Open markets matter for the well-being of countries and citizens ...

That is not to say that liberalisation is always and everywhere painless, or that one can choose to ignore its distributional or political consequences. The benefits of trade and investment liberalisation do not come without adjustment pains. Liberalisation tends to generate overall gains, but there is no denying that it does create hardship for some workers, firms and the communities in which they are located.

... but liberalisation is not painless

The key challenge for public policy in today's globalising environment is, thus, to adopt optimal strategies to spread the gains from expanded trade and investment widely in the population through structural adjustment policies designed to achieve that goal. If such gains are spread too thinly or take too long to materialise, there may be diminished political support for policies that work toward further global integration. Without a sustained effort to improve public understanding and an appropriate complementary set of domestic policies focusing on skills enhancement and aiming to smooth and shorten the "adjustment cycle" of societies, supporters of greater market openness risk a recurring backlash from those in society that are most exposed to the risks of structural change.

Staying the course of more open markets requires determined and improved efforts to improve public understanding

That said, it is important that the relative contribution of trade and investment liberalisation to ongoing structural change be properly understood, and set against other forces, chief among which is technology, that are shaping the world's economic landscape. There is a tendency to ascribe to efforts at trade and investment liberalisation a greater influence on countries' economic destinies than is warranted, relative to more purely domestic or independent forces and the exercise of sovereign policy choices. There is, similarly, a tendency to expect – and indeed promise – more from trade and investment liberalisation than either can realistically be expected to deliver.

Trade and investment liberalisation should be kept in perspective ...

Such considerations do not take away from the positive overall effects of open markets on the welfare of nations and the pocketbooks of citizens. Stated simply, more open economies typically grow faster; and faster growth and rising incomes are likely, on balance, to promote more sustainable development, facilitate adjustment and the efficient re-deployment of a society's productive resources, starting first and foremost with its human capital – its workers – while lessening political resistance to change.

... while recognising their contribution to growth and prosperity

The liberalisation debate is thus more than ever a debate over ideas, and it matters greatly that Member governments be in a position to communicate why and how market liberalisation forms part of the *answer* to the concerns of citizens, rather than being their root cause. The facts are, that five decades of multilateral co-operation have delivered the results that are highly beneficial for our citizens. Nations are now experiencing a level of widely shared and rising prosperity that few could have dared to hope for when the foundations were laid in the post-war period. What is needed now is the confidence to go forward and ensure that the future generation will also be in the position to reap the further benefits that are in prospect.

The immediacy of the pains liberalisation can generate, and the diffuse, longer-term manner in which its benefits tend to materialise for economies as a whole, will always complicate the lives of advocates of market liberalisation. However complicated, the case for open trade and investment remains profoundly compelling. Done properly, liberal trade and investment is – and must be seen as being – not only about greater prosperity and freedom of choice but also about fairness. Fairness in ensuring that the general interest – concern for the welfare of *all* citizens – prevails over special interests; and in seeing to it that the dividends of liberalisation are distributed more equitably, both within *and* between countries. This is why politics and the exercise of leadership at both the national and international level continue to matter greatly.

APPENDIX A.
THE COSTS OF PROTECTIONISM
AND THE BENEFITS OF LIBERALISATION:
ILLUSTRATIVE EXAMPLES – PAST AND PRESENT

COSTS OF PROTECTIONISM

The food you eat ...

■ The Common Agricultural Policy has been estimated to cost an average family of four around US$1,500 a year in artificially higher prices. This is the indirect cost to them as consumers; they are then charged a further US$100 per head as taxpayers to subsidise farmers directly".[1]

■ EU support for sugar producers is estimated to have cost EU consumers around 3 billion ECU a year, on average, over the period 1979-1989. This added an estimated 40 ECU per family of four per year for just this specific basic food item.[2]

■ In the early 1980s, a US program to support and protect the domestic sugar industry cost each consumer in the country about US$15.50 a year. The program included import duties and quotas.[3] In 1988, US sugar subsidies were estimated by the US Commerce Department to add an average US$3 billion a year to the grocery bill of US consumers.[4]

■ Japanese farmers received income from assistance and protection measures equivalent to a subsidy of 77 per cent of the value of production in 1995. The total cost of such measures was estimated to be Y4.640 billion, or US$49.3 billion. High levels of protection

and support, which are most significant in the case of wheat and rice production, has resulted in Japanese consumers facing very high food prices. It is estimated that 51 per cent of the price consumers paid for agricultural products in 1995 represented a tax over and above the world price.[5]

■ Import restrictions and other interventions favouring domestic producers of eggs, poultry and dairy products have resulted in significantly higher prices for consumers in Canada, Mexico and European countries. For example, in 1990 it was shown that consumers in Buffalo (US) were paying C$1.16 for a dozen large eggs while those in Toronto paid C$1.65. Milk cost C$1.23 for a half-gallon in the US and C$2.81 (2 litres) in Canada. The Buffalo consumer paid C$2.55 for a kilogram of chicken and C$4.25 for 500 grams of cheese; the same products cost C$5.03 and C$5.20 in Toronto.[6]

■ Barriers against imports of oranges were estimated to add a third to the price paid by Japanese consumers. That is also about the amount of savings which would accrue to US consumers of orange juice if US duties on Brazilian orange juice imports were abolished.[7]

■ According to estimates by the Government of New Zealand, consumers and taxpayers transferred some US$350 billion to OECD agriculture through a variety of border measures and domestic price support policies – enough to pay for each of the OECD's 41 million dairy cows to fly first class around the world one and a half times.[8]

The clothes you wear ...

■ The cost of protecting clothing production in several OECD countries has been substantial. In the late 1980s, Americans paid 58 per cent higher prices for textiles and clothing because of US trade restrictions in this sector. The cost that quotas, high tariffs or both impose on US households for clothing, was estimated at between US$8.5 billion and US$18 billion, while for textiles and clothing combined the bill reached some US$27 billion.[9]

■ Studies show that consumers in the United Kingdom and Canada in the past have had to pay an additional £500 million and C$ 780 million a year respectively for their clothing as a result of restrictions on imports of these products.[10]

■ Figures show that if 1988 tariffs still applied, Australian consumers of clothing and footwear would pay around 14 per cent more than they do today, representing an extra A$300 or so per year for the average family to maintain its dress standards.

The cars you drive ...

■ When the US limited imports of Japanese automobiles in early 1981, the price of a new US car increased by an average of 41 per cent from 1981 to 1984. This was nearly twice the average rate of increase for all consumer prices during the same period. While the industry claimed that higher prices "saved" up to 22,000 jobs, they also prevented many Americans from buying new cars. In fact, they bought around 1 million fewer cars after imports were restricted, and the drop in sales forced the auto industry to eventually lay off 50,000 workers in the late 1980s.[12]

■ Voluntary export restraints imposed by France on Japanese car imports raised prices by an estimated 33 per cent at a total cost of around US$1.7 billion in 1989. Taken together, the restrictions which France, Italy, Portugal, Spain and the United Kingdom had in place in this sector cost consumers around US$7 billion a year in higher than necessary prices.[13]

■ Figures for Australia show that imported cars would cost around 25 per cent more today if the 1988 tariffs still applied – representing an extra A$5,000 on a A$20,000 car.[14] Shielding the Australian car industry from foreign competition raises the price tag of a car bought today by A$2,900 on average.

■ If tariff protection on automobiles, clothing and footwear are added together, they would have cost in 1996, each Australian family around A$1,173 a year or A$23 per week.[15]

... and other goods and services you buy.

■ The National Consumers Council of the United Kingdom estimated that the total cost of a range of trade measures then applicable in the EU to imported consumer electronics products, such as video recorders, televisions, compact disc players and electronic typewriters, were costing EU consumers almost US$1.3 billion more a year than they would otherwise.[16]

■ In the EU, users of aluminium, including the packaging, automotive and aerospace industries, paid an extra US$472 million for the metal in 1995 because of a 6 per cent tariff charged on about 60 per cent of the aluminium imported by EU countries.[17]

The economy-wide costs of "saving" jobs through protectionism ...

■ The cost of protectionism to society often far exceeds the wages of those workers whose jobs are protected. A 1984 study by the US Federal Trade Commission estimated that then existing trade restrictions cost the US economy US$81 for every US$1 of adjustment cost saved.[18] Another study for the United States concluded that saving a single job would cost US$240,000 in the orange juice industry, US$135,000 in the ceramic tiles industry, US$420,000 in the colour TV industry, and up to US$1 million for the speciality steel industry.[19]

■ The Australian Industries Assistance Commission found that protection of the textiles, clothing and footwear industries cost A$20,000 per job in 1990, while it cost A$17,000 for every job protected in the motor vehicle industry.[20]

■ In the United States, the cost of saving a single job in the clothing sector was estimated at between US$36,000 and US$82,000 in the mid-1980s. In the United Kingdom the figure for the same year was put at £21,000.[21] In both cases, these figures exceed average industry wages by a considerable margin.

... and other food for thought.

■ In Australia, tariffs applied to various inputs which farmers need to make their living, reduce the income generated by large (broad acre) farms by A$2300 a year per farm, on average.[22]

■ Since import quotas restrict the number of products sold by foreign firms, a common reaction of the firms is to increase the value of the goods which they are allowed to send under the quotas. Research suggests that this shift by exporters of deliveries from lower- value to higher-value items, or "quality upgrading", causes a welfare cost in addition to the usual consumer welfare loss resulting from quotas. Such changes in the composition of imports to US quotas have been observed in a number of countries and industries, including steel, autos, footwear and textiles and apparel. For example, US imports of autos from Japan witnessed a very dramatic increase in their size, horsepower and luxury equipment, trade restrictions were imposed in 1981. The total dead-weight loss to the United States due to the import restriction was about US$2 billion, where this amount includes the loss caused by *both* the process and quality changes.[23] Similarly, it was observed that European firms selling cars in the United States increased their prices once Japan had agreed to limit its exports of cars to the US market in the early 1980s.[24]

■ Extensive cargo preference laws maintained by the US, which stipulate that cargo in international trade must be carried by US- flag ships, were estimated to add over US$100 million to the cost of providing food donations to foreign countries in 1985.[25]

■ It is often forgotten that customs and administrative procedures and institutions have to be set up to collect duties, distribute quotas and monitor their allocation, check products at customs for their country of origin and other special characteristics that determine applicable duty rates, etc. For certain products and countries, applied tariffs today are so low that the costs of administering them widely exceed the value of the duties collected, while their protective effect from the domestic producer's point of view is virtually zero.

■ Even if current commitments for tariff reductions are implemented as scheduled, the cost of protectionism still in place in Australia in 2,000 in terms of lost production and opportunities amount to an estimated A\$5 billion, or over A\$700 per average Australian family.[26]

BENEFITS OF LIBERALISATION

Cheaper and more varied goods ...

■ The elimination of quotas and tariffs which developed countries impose on textiles and clothing imports could generate an annual global welfare gain of around US\$23 billion. The gains could be US\$12.3 billion for the United States, \$0.8 billion for Canada, and US\$2.2 billion for the EU. In the aggregate, developing countries would gain around US\$8 billion in additional income. This latter result suggests that the economic rent transfers associated with the Multi-Fibre Arrangement (MFA) would be more than offset by the improved market access that would result from the dismantling of the MFA, which is scheduled for 2005, as a result of the Uruguay Round.[27]

■ Recent tariff reductions in Australia helped keep prices of clothing and footwear noticeably down. Since 1986-87, prices for clothing and footwear increased by around 30 per cent, whereas the Australian consumer price index (CPI) rose by a much steeper 50 per cent. Since 1991-92, prices for these products have remained virtually static. This compares with a rise of 12 per cent in the CPI over the same period.[28]

■ Households and businesses world-wide could realise annual savings worth some US\$50 billion as a result of the WTO's December 1996 Information Technology Agreement (ITA), owing to the downward pressure on prices of computers and other electronic equipment and software that should flow from the agreement. The ITA commits more than 40 countries to phasing out tariffs on a wide range of information technology products.[29]

■ The EU Single Market Programme aimed at removing remaining barriers to the free movement of goods, capital, people and services has resulted in a wider range of products and services available to public sector, industrial and domestic consumers at lower prices. For example:
– Opening Member countries' public purchasing to bidding from foreign producers instead of giving domestic companies exclusive access or preferential status on public contracts, has contributed to substantial price reductions for rolling stock used in the construction of railways (20-30 per cent reduction in prices) and equipment needed to generate and distribute power (30-40 per cent reduction).[30]
– In the automobile industry, the switch from separate national systems to a harmonised single EU approval system for authorising sales, help producers of cars save costs in research, design and development in the order of ECU 1 million per major new model. Added to that are savings from greater technical efficiency in production of components and vehicles.[31]
– The price of telecommunications equipment has fallen by an average 7 per cent from 1985 to 1995, which is equivalent to ECU 1.5-2 billion per year in additional costs to equipment purchasers in the EU. Whereas, in 1985, EU equipment prices were on average 20 per cent higher than equivalent prices in other regions of the world, this price "excess" has fallen to 8 per cent.[32]

■ Free trade broadens the range and quality of products that consumers find in the shops. For example, many fruit and vegetables are available, even out of season, throughout the year. Exotic foods, never seen just ten or twenty years ago, are now commonly found in supermarkets. Cut flowers are being transported fresh by cargo planes daily from Latin America to Europe and North America throughout the winter season.

- In the context of the US-Canada Free Trade Agreement (FTA), the prices of "un-liberalised" items for which tariffs were not removed as a result as the FTA, such as lumber or transportation equipment, were substantially higher in 1992 than in 1988, while the prices of many "liberalised" goods – paper, chemical products, iron and steel, and office equipment, among others – fell during the same period.[33]

- Signed in June 1997, a US-EU Mutual Recognition Agreement (MRA) on Conformity Assessment is expected to save US manufacturers up to 10 per cent of the cost of delivering their products to Europe.[34] According to industry estimates, the overall cost of market entry across the Atlantic will fall by US$1 billion annually, which is equivalent to a 2-3 per cent tariff cut.[35] The MRA package applies to bilateral trade in telecommunications equipment, information technology products, medical devices, pharmaceuticals and sports craft.

- Studies show that if the United States had removed all significant import restraints existing in 1993, the outcome would have been a net welfare gain for the economy of approximately $19 billion or US$74 per average household. The largest benefits from a hypothetical removal of trade barriers in 1993 would have occurred in the steel, nonrubber footwear, motor vehicle, and household audio and video equipment sectors, with combined net welfare gains totalling over US$520 million.[36] The overall welfare gain would have resulted in part from lower prices for many consumer goods, for example:

– 3.5 per cent decline on average in the price of nonrubber footwear, which includes leather and vinyl shoes, boots, sandals and slippers;
– a 2.4 per cent drop in the price of audio and video equipment, including radio and television receivers, amplifiers, speakers, video camera recorders, phonographs, audio and video tape recorders and players and compact disc players;
– a 5.5 per cent fall in the overall price of china tableware, e.g., household and commercial chinaware.

Cheaper and more varied services ...

- Liberalisation of trade in services has been associated with large reductions of prices. Prices of international phone calls have fallen at a rate of 4 per cent per annum in real terms during the 1990s in developing countries and about 2 per cent per annum in industrial countries. The World Bank predicts that the cost of a one hour transatlantic phone call could be as low as 3 cents in 2010. In the case of Japan, the price of a three-minute call to the United States dropped by 7 per cent in 1996 alone, and is expected to decline by as much as 25 per cent further by the year 2000.[37]

- Other advantages which consumers in OECD countries with competitive telecom systems have reaped in recent years over their counter-parts in countries with closed markets (on top of the direct price-advantages), include:
– a 97 per cent reduction in waiting time to obtain telecommunications service;
– a 17 per cent lower call failure rate;
– 39 per cent fewer faults per 100 lines; and
– a 34 per cent lead in number of phones digitised.[38]

- Following liberalisation of telecommunications services in the context of the EU single Market Programme, prices on international calls to the US fell on average by 42 per cent in all European countries between 1990 and

1995. Anticipation by public telephone companies of the liberalisation of infrastructures resulted in cost savings for consumers of 22.3 per cent on long distance calls. In addition, there has been a noticeable convergence in prices, as the more expensive EU countries have begun to align themselves on the prices prevailing in other EU countries. The ratio between the highest and the lowest prices for international telephone calls was reduced between 1991 and 1994 from 4 to 2.[39]

■ The WTO Agreement on Basic Telecommunication Services is expected to help realise cost savings on the order of 80 per cent for international phone calls within the next several years – from US$1 per minute on average to 20 cents.[40] According to one estimate, it could save consumers in rich and poor countries more than US$1 trillion over the next 12 years in lower charges, better service and improved technology.[41]

■ In Chile, allowing even limited competition in the telecommunications market resulted in a decline of 36 per cent in rates for local calls between 1989 and 1994, 38 per cent for long-distance calls and 50 per cent for international calls. One year after Chile opened international calls to full competition in late 1993, seven companies were offering services at rates that were down by as much as 70 per cent, placing Chilean prices for international phone calls among the lowest in the world. By late 1995, the price of a call from Chile to the United States was about four times lower than the price of a call from neighbouring Brazil to the United States and about seven time lower than one from Argentina.[42]

■ In China, the launching of mobile telecom services by Unicom – the second operator allowed to provide basic services in the domestic market – prompted the Ministry of Posts and Telecommunications to slash its mobile telephone service rates by 30 per cent. Similarly, allowing competitors to enter Ghana's domestic market for cellular services, led Mobitel, which previously enjoyed a monopoly position, to cut connection charges by 50 per cent.[43]

■ Trade and investment liberalisation in the financial services sector can boost income and growth. For example, a study of deregulation of US intrastate branching, i.e., where states relaxed restrictions on intrastate bank branching by allowing bank holding companies to consolidate bank subsidiaries into branching and permitted banks to open branches anywhere within state borders, found that this would stimulate growth by 0.3-0.9 per cent of GDP for the 10-year period following deregulation and 0.2-0.3 per cent thereafter.[44]

■ Following an initiative under the Single Market programme to liberalise financial services within the EU, the number of cross-border branches in the banking sector jumped by 58 per cent between 1993 and 1995. This means that businesses as well as individuals now have a wider choice of banks and bank services.[45]

■ Further liberalisation of international air transport services could offer large benefits. Removal in 1993 of bilateral restrictions on the free access to other EU markets for air transport services, price restrictions and slot allocations has resulted in the issuing of nearly 800 new operating licences, notably to small airlines. Thanks to lower and more flexible fares, demand for air transport has in turn risen about 20 per cent.[46]

■ In the two years following a bilateral "opening of skies" agreement between the United Kingdom and Ireland, economy fares between London and Dublin were almost halved, whereas flights between Dublin and other EU capitals remain much more expensive.[47]

■ The ongoing removal of bilateral quota restrictions on the access to other EU countries, and the elimination of delays associated with frontier controls in the road transport sector, have, so far, cut the costs of border-crossing for haulers by 5-6 per cent for a standard trip of 1000 km.[48]

Better paying and more stable jobs ...

■ The Commission of the European Communities has calculated that the Single Market Programme has resulted in between 300,000 and 900,000 more jobs than would have existed in the absence of the Single Market; an extra increase in EU income of 1.1-1.5 per cent over the period 1989-1993.[49]

■ Growth and workplace stability among exporting plants are better than among non-exporting plants. Exporting plants enjoy a striking employment growth premium. Employment growth between 1987 and 1992 at US plants that started or continued exporting during that time was 17.5 to 18.5 per cent greater than at comparable (same size and same two-digit SIC industry group) plants that did not export. Exporting plants were also 9 per cent less likely to close their doors in any given year between 1987 and 1992 than comparable non-exporting plants.[50]

■ Since 1993, exports have accounted for fully one-third of US economic growth. Today, 12 million Americans owe their jobs to exports. And nearly 2 million of those jobs were created in the past four years.[51]

■ Between 1984 and 1995, US exports to Latin America (including Mexico) grew from about US$30 billion to US$96 billion and supported about one million export-oriented jobs.[52] In the context of NAFTA, US jobs supported by exports to Canada and Mexico, which are in the higher productivity, export-oriented sectors of the economy, pay more than the US average wage. Specifically, among non-supervisory production workers, jobs in exporting sectors pay 13-16 per cent more than the US average wage.[53]

For the Irish economy, one job in four directly depended on exports in 1996.[54] For the US economy, exports of goods and services in 1994 supported directly or indirectly 1 in 10 civilian jobs. In manufacturing, the ratio was 1 in 5 jobs and in agriculture, 1 in 3.[55] In the case of Canada, 1 in 3 jobs depended on trade in 1996.[56]

■ Wages paid to employees of US foreign subsidiaries were 26 per cent higher than at all private-sector businesses in 1992.[57]

■ Modelling by the Centre for International Economics in Australia suggests that a 1 per cent increase in major agricultural, mining and manufacturing commodity exports would result in over 16,000 additional jobs within two years. Most of these additional jobs would be in service industries.[58]

■ It has been estimated for the United States that if the share of exports and imports in GDP increases by 1 per cent each, this would add US$2 to the income of each US consumer.[59]

■ Close to 30 per cent of jobs in France depend directly or indirectly on foreign direct investment.[60]

... and more food for thought.

■ In the last ten years, US exports to developing countries grew by 240 per cent – faster than exports to high-wage countries. Exports to low-wage countries now account for 42 per cent of total US exports.[61]

■ NAFTA helped limit US export losses: despite the 1994-95 peso crisis, US exports to Mexico were still $4.7 billion higher in 1995 than they were before NAFTA.

Furthermore, if Mexico had responded to the peso devaluation of 1994 in the same way as it responded to the 1982 devaluation, that is, by raising import duties to 100 per cent, imposing import licenses across the board and nationalising certain sectors of the economy, US exports would have decreased by an estimated US$20 billion.[62]

■ Between 1992 and 1996, the share of French exports to developing countries rose from 18.9 per cent to 22.2 per cent of total exports. France's trade surplus with developing countries was ten times higher that that with OECD economies during the period.[63]

■ Fully 80 per cent of French foreign direct investment is directed towards other OECD countries, suggesting that wage considerations play a relatively marginal role in shaping French firms' investment location decisions.[64]

■ The World Travel and Tourism Council estimates that tourism sustains more than one in ten jobs around the world, providing direct employment for 255 million people, and could create another 130 million places by 2006. No factors have fuelled the growth of tourism more than cheaper air travel.[65]

■ If trade liberalisation were halted at 1993 levels, wages of (US) skilled workers would decline by an estimated 2-5 per cent by the year 2013, compared with what they would be otherwise, while wages of unskilled workers would remain unchanged. If industrial countries imposed a 30 per cent tariff on all goods imported from developing countries, the results would be even worse: wages for the unskilled workers would fall 1 per cent because of higher import costs, and wages for skilled workers would drop 5 per cent. The wage gap would narrow, but only because *everybody* would get poorer.[66]

NOTES

1. See Spicer, M. (1997).
2. See Australian Bureau of Agriculture and Resource Economics (1991).
3. See "Sugar Price Rise Hits Consumer: Food, Beverage Concerns Passed Along Increase", *New York Times*, June 14, 1980, referred to in Quale, D. (1983).
4. See US Department of Commerce figures quoted in *The Wall Street Journal* (Europe), 20 July 1991.
5. See OECD (1996*c*).
6. See "Why Chickens Don't Come Cheap", in *Business Magazine*, Canada, October 1990.
7. See Bovard, J. (1991).
8. See New Zealand Ministry of Foreign Affairs and Trade (1994).
9. See Jenkins, G.P. (1980), *op.cit.;* Trade Policy Research Centre, (1984); GATT Secretariat (1993).
10. See Jenkins, G.P. (1980), *op.cit.*
11. See Commonwealth of Australia (1997), *op.cit.*
12. See Bovard, J. (1991*a*); OECD (1985); and Crandall, R.W. (1987).
13. See Smith, A. (1989).
14. See Commonwealth of Australia (1997), *op. cit.*
15. See Commonwealth of Australia (1997) *op.cit.*
16. See *International Trade: The Consumer Agenda*, National Consumer Council, London, 1993.
17. Statement by Jean-Pierre Ergas, Executive Vice-President of Alacan Aluminum of Canada, quoted in "Call for Abolition of EU Aluminium Tariffs", *The Financial Times*, 24 June 1997.
18. See Tarr, D. and Morkre, M. (1984).
19. See Crandall, R.W. (1987), *op.cit.*
20. See Center for International Economics (1993).
21. See Crandall, R.W. (1987).
22. See Commonwealth of Australia (1997), *op.cit.*
23. See Winston, C. and Associates (1987).
24. See Dinopoulos, E. and Kreinin, M. (1988).
25. See US General Accounting Office, June 1985.
26. See Commonwealth of Australia (1997), *op.cit.*
27. See Trela, I. and Whalley, J. (1991).
28. See Commonwealth of Australia (1997), *op.cit.*
29. Estimates of the Washington-based Institute for International Economics, cited in "Consumer Group Recommends Items for ITA", *International Trade Reporter*, November 27, 1996.
30. See Commission of the European Communities (1996*c*).
31. See Commission of the European Communities (1996*b*).
32. See Commission of the European Communities (1996*a*).
33. See Schwanen, D. (1993).

34. See US Trade Representative (1997).
35. Under Secretary of Commerce for International Trade, Timothy Hauser in testimony before the House of Representatives' Ways and Means Trade Subcommittee on 23 July 1997. "Hauser on US-European Trade Relations", hhtp://www.insidetrade.com/sec-cgi/as_web.exe?SEC_world17+D+2207700, 26 September 1997.
36. See US International Trade Commission (1995), *op.cit.*
37. See "2 Japan Phone Firms are Planning to Merge", in *International Herald Tribune*, 13 March 1997.
38. See Petrazzini, B. (1996).
39. See Commission of the European Communities (1996*d*).
40. See "Basic Telecom Negotiations", Statement of Ambassador Charlene Barshefsky, 15 February 1997, http://ustr.gov/agreements/telecom/barshefsky.html
41. Figures of the Institute for International Economics cited in "WTO's Telecom Pact Promises to Speed Pace of Global Liberalization", in *Wall Street Journal* (Europe), February 14, 1997
42. See Petrazzini, B. (1996), *op.cit.*
43. See Petrazzini, B. (1996), *op.cit.*
44. See Jayaratne, J. and Strahan, P.E. (1996).
45. See OECD (1997), p. 308.
46. See Commission of the European Communities (1996), *op.cit.*
47. See Hufbauer, G.C. and Findley, C., eds. (1996).
48. See Commission of the European Communities (1996d).
49. See Commission of the European Communities (1996), *op.cit.*
50. See Richardson, J.D. and Rindal, K. (1996).
51. See Daley, W. (1998).
52. Remarks by Ambassador Stuart Eizenstat, Under Secretary of Commerce for International Trade, at Salud-America 1996 Conference, San Diego, California, 11 July 1996.
53. See USTR (1997*a*).
54. See Government of Ireland (1998).
55. See US Department of Commerce (1997*a*).
56. See Government of Canada (1997).
57. See OFII (1997).
58. See OFII (1997), *op.cit.*
59. See Romer, D. and Frankel, J. A. (1997).
60. Statement by French Finance Minister Dominique Strauss-Kahn before the country's National Assembly, as reported in "Cet AMI nous veut-il du mal?", *Le Figaro*, (15 February 1998).
61. See Daley, W. (1998), *op.cit.*
62. See Paul Dacher, The North American Free Trade Agreement (NAFTA): A Status Report, Business America, August 1996, p.10.
63. See Ruggiero, R. (1998), "La France ne doit pas craindre la mondialisation", in *Le Figaro*, (17 February).
64. See Ruggiero, R. (1998), *op.cit.*
65. See "Dream Factories" (A survey of travel and tourism), in *The Economist*, 10 January 1998.
66. See Cline, W. (1997).

APPENDIX B.
BANKING SECTOR LIBERALISATION AND FINANCIAL CRISES

While it may be premature to attempt to draw the full lessons from the Asian turmoil, a strong case can be made that greater market access of foreign banks might have helped to mitigate the crisis. A common theme which emerges in all affected economies is that of a poorly-regulated and under-performing financial sector, where foreign entry was circumscribed or prohibited. Local banks have often functioned as instruments of government industrial policy, rather than as independent entities which lend prudently and channel credit to its most efficient uses.

Although host countries have often been reluctant to admit foreign banks on the same terms and conditions as local banks (i.e., afford them so-called "national treatment"), the arguments in favour of greater liberalisation in this sector are not fundamentally different from those applying to other sectors. Foreign banks introduce new financial products and bring with them technology, competitive management techniques and experience in risk management and credit analysis. The presence of foreign banks might also introduce a greater degree of competition into what is often a "cosy oligopoly", too often characterised by political interference and unsound cross-shareholding practices involving banks and industrial enterprises. As a result, studies have found that allowing foreign bank entry improves standards, and that open financial systems are more efficient and offer better services.[1]

Of most relevance to countries faced with financial vulnerability, foreign banks are less likely to concentrate their lending on a small number of local firms, and they can draw on the capital of the parent company if there are liquidity problems. Foreign banks have often proved to be a stable source of funding in the face of adverse shocks in many countries, particularly developing ones.[2]

Contrary to the claim that rapid expansion of the presence of foreign banks in a host economy undermines attempts at regulation, it is more likely that this presence will help to improve transparency and overall banking regulation in the host country. A recent study argues that foreign banks exert pressure for improved regulation and supervision, better disclosure rules, general improvements in the legal and regulatory framework for the provision of financial services, and improved credibility of rules as the country enters into international agreements and intensifies linkages with foreign regulators.[3] A sound regulatory framework for financial sector supervision is thus a necessary complement to trade and investment liberalisation.

NOTES

1. See Claessens, S. and Glaessner, T. (1997).
2. See Group of Ten (G-10) (1997).
3. See Claessens, S. and Glaessner, T. (1997), *op.cit.*

APPENDIX C.
ESTIMATING THE GAINS FROM THE URUGUAY ROUND

The Uruguay Round agreements represent the most thorough reform of the world trading system since the establishment of the General Agreement on Tariffs and Trade in 1947. The agreements continued the trend of widening the multilateral trading system's negotiating agenda and increasing the number of participating countries. The agreements broke new ground by extending the application of multilateral rules to trade in agricultural products and textiles and clothing, areas that were largely outside GATT disciplines or governed by special arrangements. In addition, the General Agreement on Trade in Services (GATS) and agreements on trade-related intellectual property rights (TRIPs) and trade-related investment measures (TRIMs), significantly broadened the coverage of multilateral trade rules. Such changes reflect the trading system's adaptation to a rapidly globalising world economy. Moreover, with the establishment of the World Trade Organization, new mechanisms for reviewing trade policies, implementing rules and settling disputes among trading partners were introduced.

The Uruguay Round resulted in significant tariff reductions on industrial goods. Developed countries agreed to reduce their bound tariffs on manufactures (weighted by trade shares) from 6.3 per cent on average, to 3.9 per cent over the course of the Round's implementation period, an almost 40 per cent reduction. Developing countries also agreed to reduce their tariffs from an average of 15.3 per cent to 12.3 per cent, a 30 per cent decline.

These results exceed the depth of the tariff cuts achieved in previous negotiating rounds. Equally important, the Uruguay Round witnessed a sharp increase – from 22 per cent when it was launched in 1986 to 72 per cent when it concluded in 1993 – in the share of developing country tariff lines that are now multilaterally bound.

"How much is this all worth?" is a natural question to ask. It also happens to be a difficult one to answer precisely. Several studies estimate that substantial gains in global income will accrue from the liberalisation achieved under the Round (see below). However, the results of these studies vary because of differences in methodology and specification of economic models. Still, they can be used to suggest some broad order of magnitudes.

Work by the WTO suggests annual gains to global income of $94 billion in 1992 US dollars, from liberalisation in merchandise trade alone[1]. If, as can be expected, liberalisation also results in higher levels of investment, these gains could be as large as $214 billion annually, or almost 1 per cent of the value of global output in 1992. The WTO results also show that roughly half of these additional gains should accrue to developing countries. Other studies yield similar estimates of gains. Simulations, which assume a starting point of unemployment, yield much larger estimates of gains, including better capacity utilisation and greater overall resource use.

A World Bank study includes the effects of scale economies as well as induced investment.[2]

**Estimated welfare gains from the Uruguay Round
(billions of US dollars annually in 1992 prices)**

Model	Variant	World	Developed	Developing
WTO (1994)	Static, perfect competition	40	30	10
from 1992	Static, imperfect competition	94	75	19
	With induced investment	214	121	93
World Bank (1995)	Static, perfect competition	93	179	56
from 1992	Static, imperfect competition	96	75	18
	With induced investment	171	77	19
World Bank/OECD Development Centre (1993) from 2002	Starting from full employment	48	32	16
	Starting with unemployment	235	179	56
OECD (1993) from 2002	Perfect competition	274	188	86

These suggest gains that raise world income by $171 billion in 1992 US dollars, with a third going to developing countries. Meanwhile, work carried out by the OECD suggests gains in aggregate welfare ranging from $235 to $274 billion in 1992 US dollars (measured in 2002). [3] OECD estimates show that between a quarter to a third of the welfare gains arising from the Uruguay Round are reaped by developing countries.[4] Of considerable importance to this study is the finding that welfare gains are, to an important degree, proportionate to each country's own liberalisation efforts. Simply stated, countries that do the most by eliminating or reducing distortions and discriminatory practices, register larger welfare gains relative to others.

To put the latter figures into perspective, the measured economic effect of the Uruguay Round can be seen as roughly equivalent to adding the GDP of a new Switzerland or Korea to the world economy by 2005. Of course, no assessment of an undertaking as complex as the Uruguay Round can ever be precise, and it bears recalling that many of its potential benefits defy quantification, such as the effects of greater transparency and security of market access or strengthened dispute settlement procedures. This is also the case of disciplines and liberalisation commitments in areas such as standards, services, investment and intellectual property, whose benefits can only be gauged somewhat impressionistically. By focusing, albeit imperfectly, on what is measurable, available studies may thus actually underestimate the dynamic gains the multilateral trading system can potentially deliver to nations and their citizens.

NOTES

1. See François, J., MacDonald, B. and Nordstrom, H. (1995).

2. See Harrison, G., Rutherford, T. and Tarr, D. (1995).

3. See Goldin, Knudsen, I.O., and van der Mensbrugghe, D. (1993).

4. The higher of the two figures reflects the additional effects of cuts in non-tariff barriers on industrial products.

BIBLIOGRAPHY

AUSTRALIAN BUREAU OF AGRICULTURE AND RESOURCE ECONOMICS (1991), *Domestic and World Market Effects of EC Sugar Policies*, Commonwealth of Australia, Canberra.

ADAMS, J. (1997), "Globalisation, Trade and Environment", *Globalisation and Environment: Preliminary Perspectives*, OECD, Paris.

AITKEN, B., HANSON, G.D., and HARRISON, A. (1994), *"Spillovers, Foreign Investment and Export Behavior"*, NBER Working Paper No. 4967, NBER (December), Cambridge, Massachusetts.

BAILY, M.N. (1993), "Competition, Regulation and Efficiency in Service Industries", *Brookings Papers on Economic Activity - Microeconomics*, No. 2.

BAILY, M.N. and GERSBACH, H. (1995), "Efficiency in Manufacturing and the Need for Global Competition", *Brookings Papers on Economic Activity - Microeconomics*, No. 1.

BARRETT, S. (1993), "Strategic Environmental Policy and International Competitiveness", *Environmental Policies and Industrial Competitiveness*, OECD, Paris.

BERNARD, A.B. and Jensen, J.B. (1997), *"Exceptional Exporter Performance: Cause, Effect or Both?"*, NBER Working Paper 6272 (November), National Bureau of Economic Research, Cambridge, Massachusetts.

BHAGWATI, J. (1988), *Protectionism*, MIT Press, Cambridge, Massachusetts.

BIRDSALL, N. and WHEELER, D. (1993), "Trade Policy and Pollution in Latin America: Where are the Pollution Havens?", *Journal of Environment and Development*, Vol. 2, No. 1, (Winter), pp. 137-49.

BIS (1997), *67th Annual Report*, Bank for International Settlements, Basel.

BLAZEICZAK, J. (1993), "Environmental Policies and Foreign Investment: The Case of Germany", *Environmental Policies and Industrial Competitiveness*, OECD, Paris.

BLOMSTROM, M. and A. KOKKO (1997*), "The Impact of Foreign Investment on Host Countries: A Review of the Empirical Evidence"*, Policy Research Working Papers No. 1745, (March), World Bank, Washington, DC.

BORENSZTEIN, E., de GREGORIO, J. and LEE, J. (1995), *"How Does Foreign Investment Affect Economic Growth?"*, NBER Working Paper 5057, National Bureau of Economic Research, Cambridge, Massachusetts.

BOVARD, J. (1991), "The Myth of Fair Trade", *Policy Analysis*, No. 164, (November), Cato Institute, Washington, DC.

BOVARD, J. (1991a), *The Fair Trade Fraud*, St. Martin's Press, New York.

CAVES, R. *et al.* (1992), *Industrial Efficiency in Six Nations*, MIT Press., Cambridge, Massachusetts.

CENTER FOR INTERNATIONAL ECONOMICS (1993), *Let's Talk Tariffs*, Center for International Economics, Canberra.

CLAESSENS, S. and GLAESSNER, T. (1997), *"Internationalisation of financial services in Asia"*, mimeo, (November), World Bank, Washington, DC.

CLINE, W. (1997), *Trade and Income Distribution*, Institute for International Economics, Washington, DC.

COE, D., HELPMAN, E. and HOFFMAISTER, A. (1995), *North-South R&D Spillovers*, CEPR Discussion Paper 1133, CEPR, London.

COMMISSION OF THE EUROPEAN COMMUNITIES (1996), *The 1996 Single Market Review*, *Commission Staff Working Paper*, Commission of the European Communities, Brussels (December).

COMMISSION OF THE EUROPEAN COMMUNITIES (1996a), "Telecommunications Equipment", *The Single Market Review Series, Sub-series I - Impact on Manufacturing,* Commission of the European Communities, Brussels (August).

COMMISSION OF THE EUROPEAN COMMUNITIES (1996b), "Motor Vehicles", in *The Single Market Review Series, Sub-series I - Impact on Manufacturing,* Commission of the European Communities, Brussels (November).

COMMISSION OF THE EUROPEAN COMMUNITIES (1996c), *The Impact and Effectiveness of the Single Market*, (October), Communication from the Commission to the European Parliament and Council, Commission of the European Communities, Brussels.

COMMISSION OF THE EUROPEAN COMMUNITIES (1996d), "Telecommunications: Liberalised Services", in *The Single Market Review Series, Sub-series II - Impact on Services*, (August), Commission of the European Communities, Brussels.

COMMISSION OF THE EUROPEAN COMMUNITIES (1996e), "Road Freight Transport", in *The Single Market Review Series, Sub-series II - Impact on Services* (March), Commission of the European Communities, Brussels.

COMMISSION OF THE EUROPEAN COMMUNITIES (1994), *Trade and Investment - Discussion Paper*, Unit for Analysis and Policy Planning, Directorate General for External Economic Relations, Commission of the European Communities, Brussels.

COMMONWEALTH OF AUSTRALIA (1997), *Trade Liberalisation*: Opportunities for Australia, Foreign Affairs and Trade, Canberra: Commonwealth of Australia.

CRANDALL, W. R. (1987), "The Effects of US Trade Protection for Autos and Steel", in *Brookings Papers on Economic Activity,* No. 1.

DACHER, P. (1996), "The North American Free Trade Agreement (NAFTA): A Status Report", in *Business America*, (August).

DALEY, W. (1998), *"Building the Case for Open Trade"*, Remarks delivered at the John F. Kennedy School of Government, Harvard University (10 February), Cambridge, Massachusetts.

DASGUPTA, S. *et al.* (1995), *"Environmental Regulation and Development: A Cross-Country Empirical Analysis"*, Policy Research Working Paper 1448, World Bank, (April), Washington, DC.

DASGUPTA, S., MODY, A. and SINHA, S. (1995*), "Japanese Multinationals in Asia: Capabilities and Motivations"*, World Bank Working Paper, World Bank, Washington, DC.

DAVIS, L. A. (1996), *U.S. Jobs Supported by Goods and Services Exports, 1983-94*, Research Series OIMA-1-96, U.S. Department of Commerce, (November), Washington, DC.

DINOPOULOS, E. and KREININ, M. (1988), "Effects of the US-Japan VER on European prices and on US Welfare", *The Review of Economics and Statistsics*, Vol. 70, No. 3, (August), pp. 484-91.

EDWARDS, S. (1993), "Openness, Trade Liberalization and Growth in Developing Countries", *Journal of Economic Literature*, Vol. 32, pp. 1359-93.

ESTY, D.C. and GENTRY, B.S., (1997), "Foreign Investment, Globalisation and Environment", in OECD *Globalisation and Environment: Preliminary Perspectives,* OECD, Paris.

FLORIDA, R., "Foreign Direct Investment and the Economy" in Beltz, C.A., ed. (1995), *The Foreign Investment Debate: Opening Markets Abroad or Closing Markets at Home?,* pp. 63-95, The American Enterprise Institute Press, Washington, DC.

FLIESS, B. and SAUVÉ, P. (1998), *"Of Chips, Floppy Disks and Great Timing: Assessing the WTO Information Technology Agreement"*, Paper prepared for the Institut Français des Relations Internationales and the Tokyo Club Foundation for Global Studies, (January), available at http://www.tcf.or.jp/

FONTAGNÉ, L. (1997), *"How Foreign Investment Affects International Trade and Competitiveness: An International Assessment"*, Paper prepared for the OECD Industry Committee, (21 October), OECD, Paris.

FRANÇOIS, MACDONALD, J. B. and NORDSTROM, H. (1995), "Assessing the Uruguay Round", in Martin, W. and Winters, L. A., eds., *The Uruguay Round and the Developing Economies*, World Bank Discussion Paper No. 307, pp. 117-214, World Bank, Washington, DC.

FRANKEL, J.A. and SCHMUKLER, S.L. (1996), "Country Fund Discounts and the Mexican Crisis of December 1994", in *International Finance Discussion Papers*, 563, (September).

GARROD, B. (1997), "Business Strategies, Globalisation and Environment", *Globalisation and Environment: Preliminary Perspectives*, OECD, Paris.

GASTON, N. and TREFLER, D. (1997), "The Labour Market Consequences of the Canada-US Free Trade Agreement", in *Canadian Journal of Economics,* (February), pp. 18-41.

GATT (1993), *Secretariat Study* for *GATT Textiles Committee*, General Agreement on Tariffs and Trade, (April), Geneva.

GATT (1993a), *"Trade, the Uruguay Round and the Consumer: The Sting - How Governments Buy Votes on Trade with the Consumer's Money"*, Press Release, General Agreement on Tariffs and Trade, (11 August), Geneva.

GENTRY, B.S. *et.al.* (1996), *Private Capital Flows and the Environment: Lessons from Latin America*, mimeo, Yale Centre for Environmental Law and Policy, New Haven, Connecticut.

GOLDIN, I., KNUDSEN, O., and VAN DER MENSBRUGGHE, D. (1993), *Trade Liberalisation: Global Economic Implications*, World Bank, Washington, DC and OECD Development Centre, Paris.

GOVERNMENT OF CANADA (1997), *Small Business Quarterly*, (Fall), Industry Canada, Ottawa.

GOVERNMENT OF CANADA (1997a), *Canada's International Market Access Priorities - 1997*, Department of Foreign Affairs and International Trade, Ottawa.

GOVERNMENT OF IRELAND (1998), *Statement of National Trade Policy,* Department of Enterprise, Trade and Employment, Dublin.

GRAHAM, E.M. and KRUGMAN, P. (1995), *Foreign Direct Investment in the United States*, Third Edition, Institute for International Economics, Washington, DC.

GREENAWAY, D. *et. al.* (1989), "Empirical Evidence on Trade Orientation and Economic Performance in Developing Countries", *CREDIT Working Paper* 89/3, University of Nottingham.

GROSSMAN, G. and KRUEGER, A.B. (1992), "Environmental Impacts of a North American Free Trade Agreement", *CEPR Discussion Paper No. 644*, Centre for Economic Policy Research, London.

GROUP OF TEN (G-10) (1997), "Financial Stability in Emerging Market Economies: A Strategy for the Formulation, Adoption and Implementation of Sound Principles and Practices to Strengthen Financial Systems", *Report of the Working Party on Financial Stability in Emerging Market Economies*, Bank for International Settlements, Basel.

HARRISON, G.W., RUTHERFORD, T.F. and TARR, D.G. (1995), "Quantifying the Uruguay Round", in Martin, W. and Winters, L.A., eds., *The Uruguay Round and the Developing Economies*, World Bank Discussion Paper No. 307, World Bank, Washington, DC.

HOEKMAN, B. and KOTESCKI, M. (1995), *The Political Economy of the World Trading System: From GATT to WTO*, Oxford University Press, Oxford.

HUFBAUER, G. C. (1996), "Surveying the Costs of Protection: A Partial Equilibrium Approach", in Schott, J.J. ed., *The World Trading System: Challenges Ahead,* pp. 27-39, Institute for International Economics, Washington, DC.

HUFBAUER, G. C. and FINDLEY, C. eds. (1996), *Flying High: Liberalisating Civil Aviation in the Asia Pacific*, Institute for International Economics, Washington DC.

IMF (1997), *World Economic Outlook - May 1997*, International Monetary Fund, Washington, DC.

IMF (1995), *International Capital Markets: Developments, Prospects and Policy Issues, (August).* International Monetary Fund, Washington, DC.

INTERNATIONAL FINANCE CORPORATION (1997), *Foreign Direct Investment: Lessons of Experience*, World Bank, Washington, DC.

JACOBSON, L.S., LALONDE, R.J., and SULLIVAN, D.G. (1993), "Earnings Losses of Displaced Workers", in *American Economic Review* 83, pp. 685-709.

JAYARATNE, J. and STRAHAN, P.E. (1996), "The Finance-growth Nexus: Evidence from Bank Branch Deregulation", in *Quarterly Journal of Economics*, 111, pp. 639-670.

JENKINS, G.P. (1980), "*Costs and Consequences of the New Protectionism: The Case of Canada's Clothing Sector*", North South Institute, Ottawa.

JOHNSTONE, N. (1997*),* "Globalisation, Technology and Environment", *Globalisation and Environment: Preliminary Perspectives*, OECD, Paris.

KEOHANE, R.O. (1998), "International Institutions: Can Interdependence Work?", in *Foreign Policy,* No.110, (Spring), pp. 82-96.

KRUEGER, A. O. (1978), *Foreign Trade Regimes and Economic Development: Liberalization Attempts and Consequences*, Ballinger, Cambridge, Massachusetts.

LAWRENCE, R.Z. and LITAN, R.E. (1997), "*Globaphobia: The Wrong Debate Over Trade Policy",* in Brookings Policy Brief No. 24, Brookings Institution, Washington, DC.

LAWRENCE, R.Z. (1996), *Single World, Divided Nations? International Trade and OECD Labor Markets*, Brookings Institution, Washington, DC and OECD Development Centre, Paris.

LAWRENCE, R.Z. and SLAUGHTER, M. (1993), "International Trade and American Wages in the 1980s: Giant Sucking Sound or Small Hiccup?", in *Brookings Papers on Economic Activity: Microeconomics,* No. 2, pp. 161-226.

LOW, P. and YEATS, A. (1992).,"Do Dirty Industries Migrate?", in Low, P. ed., *International Trade and the Environment,* World Bank Discussion Paper No. 159, World Bank, Washington, DC.

LUCAS, R., WHEELER, D. and HEITIGE, H. (1992), "Economic Development, Environmental Regulation and International Migration of Toxic Pollution", in Low, P., ed., *International Trade and the Environment,* World Bank Discussion Paper No. 159, World Bank, Washington, DC.

MANI, M. and WHEELER, D. (1997), *"In Search of Pollution Havens? Dirty Industries in the World Economy, 1960-95"*, mimeo, Policy Research Department, World Bank, Washington, DC.

MCKINNEY, J. A. and ROWLEY, K.A. (1986), "The Economic Impact of the Japanese Automobile Export Restraint", in *Atlantic Economic Journal*, Vol. 14, No. 2, (July) , pp. 9-15.

NEVEN, D. and C. WYPLOSZ (1996), "Relative Prices, Trade and Restructuring in European Industry", *Centre for Economic Policy Research Working Paper No. 1451*, CEPR, London.

NEW ZEALAND MINISTRY OF FOREIGN AFFAIRS AND TRADE (1994), *Trading Ahead - The GATT Uruguay Round: Results for New Zealand*, Government of New Zealand, Auckland.

NG, F. and YEATS, A. (1996), "Open Economies Work Better! Did Africa's Protectionist Policies Cause its Marginalization in World Trade*?"*, *Policy Research Working Paper 1636*, World Bank, Washington, DC.

OECD (1998), *Agricultural Policies in OECD Countries: Monitoring and Evaluation*, Paris.

OECD (1998a), *Financial Market Trends*, No. 69, Paris.

OECD (1997), *Labour Force Statistics,* Paris.

OECD (1997a), *Historical Statistics,* Paris

OECD (1997b), *Employment Outlook 1997,* Paris.

OECD (1997c), *International Direct Investment Statistics Yearbook*, Paris.

OECD (1997d), *Globalisation and Small and Medium Enterprises*, Paris

OECD (1997e), "Financial Sector Liberalisation in Emerging Markets", *Economic Outlook*, No. 61, Paris.

OECD (1997f), *"Internationalisation of Industrial R&D: Patterns and Trends"*, Industry Committee, Paris.

OECD (1997g), *Globalisation and Linkages to 2020: Can Poor Countries and Poor People Prosper in the New Global Age,* Paris.

OECD (1997*h*), *Implementing the OECD Jobs Strategy: Member Countries' Experience*, Paris.

OECD (1997*i*), *Implementing the OECD Jobs Strategy: Lessons from Member Countries' Experience*, Paris.

OECD (1997*j*), *Globalisation and Environment: Preliminary Perspectives*, Paris.

OECD (1997*k*), *Report on Regulatory Reform, Vol II: Thematic Studies*, Paris.

OECD (1997*l*), *The World in 2020: Towards a New Global Age*, Paris.

OECD (1997*m*), Communique of the Meeting of the Council at Ministerial Level, (26-27 May), Paris.

OECD (1997*n*), *The Uruguay Round Agreement on Agricultural and Processed Agricultural Products,* Paris.

OECD (1996), *The Performance of Foreign Affiliates in OECD Countries,* Paris.

OECD (1996*a*), *Technology and Industrial Performance*, Paris.

OECD (1996*b*), *Trade, Employment and Labour Standards: A Study of Core Workers' Rights and International Trade,* Paris.

OECD (1996*c*), *Agricultural Policies, Markets and Trade: Monitoring and Evaluation,* Paris.

OECD (1995), *The New Financial Landscape: Forces Shaping the Revolution in Banking, Risk Management and Capital Markets*, Paris.

OECD (1995*a*), *Report on Trade and Environment to the OECD Council at Ministerial Level*, Paris.

OECD (1995*b*), *Foreign Direct Investment, Trade and Employment,* Paris.

OECD (1995*c*), *The Uruguay Round: A Preliminary Evaluation of the Impacts of the Agreement on Agriculture in the OECD countries,* Paris.

OECD (1994), *The OECD Jobs Study: Evidence and Explanations*, Paris.

OECD (1994*a*), *The Environmental Effects of Trade*, Paris.

OECD (1993), *Environmental Policies and Industrial Competitiveness*, Paris.

OECD (1993*a*), *Assessing the Effects of the Uruguay Round*, Trade Policy Issues No. 2, Trade Directorate, Paris.

OECD (1985), *Costs and Benefits of Protection*, Paris.

OFII (1997), *International Investment in the United States,* Organisation for International Investment, Washington, DC.

OSTRY, S. (1996), "Technology Issues in the International Trading System", in *Market Access After the Uruguay Round: Trade, Investment and Competition Perspectives*, pp. 145-70, OECD, Paris.

PAPADEMETRIOU, D.G. (1998), "Migration: Think Again", *Foreign Policy, No. 109, pp. 15-31.*

PAPAGEORGIOU, D., MICHAELY, M., and CHOSKI, A. (1990), "Liberalizing Foreign Trade in Developing Countries", in *Lessons of Experience in the Developing World*, Vol. 7, Basil Blackwell for The World Bank, Oxford.

PETRAZZINI, B. (1996), *Global Telecom Talks: A Trillion Dollar Deal*, Institute for International Economics (June), Washington DC.

PILAT, D. (1996), "Competition, Productivity and Efficiency", in *OECD Economic Studies*, Vol. 27, No. 2, pp. 107-46, OECD, Paris.

QUAYLE, D. (1983), "United States International Competitiveness and Trade Policies for the 1980s", *Northwestern Journal of International Law and Business,* Vol.5, No.1, (Spring).

RAVENGA, A. (1992), "Exporting Jobs? The Impact of Import Competition on Employment and Wages in U.S. Manufacturing", in *Quarterly Journal of Economics*, (February), pp. 255-84.

RICHARDSON, J.D. and RINDAL, K. (1996), *Why Exports Really Matter - Mor*e!, Institute for International Economics and The Manufacturing Institute, Washington, DC.

RICHARDSON, J.D. *et al.* (1998), "U.S. Performance and Trade Strategy in a Shifting Global Economy", in Feketekuty, G. and Stokes, B., eds. *Trade Strategies for a New Era: Ensuring U.S. Leadership in a Global Economy*, pp. 39-64, Council on Foreign Relations and the Monterey Institute of International Studies, New York.

RODRIK, D. (1997), *Has Globalisation Gone Too Far?,* Institute for International Economics, Washington, DC.

RODRIK, D., (1996), "Labor Standards in International Trade: Do They Matter and What Do We Do About Them?", in Lawrence, R.Z., Whalley, J. and Rodrik, D., *Emerging Agenda for Global Trade: High Stakes for Developing Countries*, Policy Essay No. 20, pp. 35-80, Overseas Development Council, Washington, DC.

ROMER, D. and FRANKEL, J.A. (1997), *"Trade and Growth: An Empirical Investigation",* NBER Working Paper No. 5476 (March), National Bureau of Economic Research, Cambridge, Massachusetts.

SACHS, J. (1998), "International Economics: Unlocking the Mysteries of Globalization", in *Foreign Policy,* No. 110, (Spring), pp. 97-111.

SACHS, J. and SHATZ H. (1994), "Trade and Jobs in US Manufacturing", in *Brookings Paper on Economic Activity,* pp. 1-84.

SAINT-PAUL, G. (1994), *"Trade Patterns and Pollution"*, Working Paper 40.94, Fondazione Eni Enrico, Mattei, Milan.

SPICER, M. (1997), "Europe's Agricultural Debacle" in *The Wall Street Journal (Europe)*, (30 October).

SCHMIDHEINY, S. and Business Council for Sustainable Development (1992), *Changing Course: A Global Business Perspective on Development and the Environment,* MIT Press, Cambridge, Massachusetts.

SCHWANEN, D. (1993), "A Growing Success: Canada's Performance Under Free Trade", in *C. D. Howe Commentary*, No. 52, C.D. Howe Institute, Toronto.

SELDON, T.M. and SONG, D. (1994), "Environmental Quality and Development: Is There a Kuznets Curve for Air Pollution Emissions?"in *Journal of Environmental Economics*, Vol. 27, pp. 147-62.

SLAUGHTER, M. and SWAIGEL, P. (1997), "The Effect of Globalization on Wages in the Industrial Countries in IMF", *Staff Studies for the World Economic Outlook*, International Monetary Fund, Washington, DC.

SMITH, A. (1989), *"The Market for Cars in the Enlarged European Community"*, CEPR, London.

SORSA, P. (1994), *"Competitiveness and Environmental Standards: Some Exploratory Results"*, Policy Research Working Paper 1249, World Bank, Washington, DC.

TARR, D. and M. MORKRE (1984), *Aggregate Cost to the United States of Tariffs and Quotas on Imports*, United States Federal Trade Commission, Washington DC.

TRADE POLICY RESEARCH CENTRE (1984), *Cost of Protecting Jobs in Textiles and Clothing,* Trade Policy Research Centre, London.

TRELA, I. and WHALLEY, J. (1991), "Internal Quota Allocation Schemes and the Costs of the MFA", in *National Bureau of Economic Research Working Papers,* No. 3627, (February).

UNCTAD (1997), *World Investment Report 1997 - Transnational Corporations, Market Structure and Competition Policy*, UNCTAD, Geneva.

UNCTAD (1996), *World Investment Report 1996 - Investment, Trade and International Policy Arrangements*, UNCTAD, Geneva.

UNCTAD (1996a), *Sharing's Asia's Dynamism: Asian Direct Investment in the European Union*, UNCTAD, Geneva.

UNCTAD (1994), Environmental Management in Transnational Corporations: *Report on the Benchmark Environment Survey*, United Nations, Geneva.

UNITED NATIONS CENTRE ON TRANSNATIONAL CORPORATIONS (1992), *The Determinants of Foreign Direct Investment: A Survey of the Evidence,* UNCTC Current Series, New York.

US DEPARTMENT OF COMMERCE (1997), *Foreign Direct Investment in the United States*, Washington, D.C. (November), available at http://www.domino.stat-usa.gov/selected/ch1-5.htm

US DEPARTMENT OF LABOR (1996), *Employment and Wages in Foreign-Owned Businesses in the United States, Fourth Quarter 1992*, Bureau of Labour Statistics, Washington, DC. (October).

US INTERNATIONAL TRADE COMMISSION (1997*), The Dynamic Effects of Trade Liberalization: An Empirical Analysis*, Investigation No.-332-375, Publication 3069, Washington, DC (October), available at http://www.usitc.gov/332S/ES3069.htm

US INTERNATIONAL TRADE COMMISSION (1995), *The Economic Effects of Significant US Import Restraint - First Biannual Update*, Washington, DC.

US TRADE REPRESENTATIVE (1997), "*US-EU Achieve Breakthrough on MRA Negotiations*", Press Release, 28 May 1997, US Trade Representative, Washington, DC.

US TRADE REPRESENTATIVE (1997*a), Study on the Operation and Effects of the North American Free Trade Agreement,* Report to the Congress of the United States, (July), Office of the US Trade Representative, Washington, DC.

WINSTON, C. and Associates (1987), *Blind Intersection? Policy and the Automobile Industry.* Brookings Institution, Washington, DC.

WORLD BANK (1995), *World Development Report 1995 - Workers in an Integrating World,* World Bank, Washington, DC.

WTO (1997), *Annual Report*, World Trade Organization, Geneva.

WTO (1997*a), Economic Effects of Services Trade Liberalization,* (October), World Trade Organization, Geneva.

WTO (1995), *Trading into the Future*, World Trade Organization, Geneva

OECD PUBLICATIONS
2, rue André-Pascal, 75775 PARIS CEDEX 16
PRINTED IN FRANCE
(2298011P) - ISBN 92-64-16100-7 – N° 50257 1998